YOU'RE THE
BOSS

GROWING AND SELLING A SUCCESSFUL
CONSULTING FIRM

YOU'RE THE
BOSS

GROWING AND SELLING A SUCCESSFUL CONSULTING FIRM

Raj Aseervatham

CRC Press
Taylor & Francis Group
Boca Raton   London   New York

CRC Press is an imprint of the
Taylor & Francis Group, an **informa** business

A PRODUCTIVITY PRESS BOOK

CRC Press
Taylor & Francis Group
6000 Broken Sound Parkway NW, Suite 300
Boca Raton, FL 33487-2742

© 2016 by Raj Aseervatham
CRC Press is an imprint of Taylor & Francis Group, an Informa business

No claim to original U.S. Government works

Printed on acid-free paper
Version Date: 20160113

International Standard Book Number-13: 978-1-4987-5189-6 (Hardback)

Library of Congress Cataloging-in-Publication Data

Names: Aseervatham, Raj, author.
Title: You're the boss : growing and selling a successful consulting firm / Raj Aseervatham.
Description: Boca Raton, FL : CRC Press, 2016. | Includes bibliographical references and index.
Identifiers: LCCN 2015046009 | ISBN 9781498751896 (alk. paper)
Subjects: LCSH: Consulting firms--Management. | Small business--Growth. | Sale of business enterprises.
Classification: LCC HD69.C6 A726 2016 | DDC 001--dc23
LC record available at http://lccn.loc.gov/2015046009

Visit the Taylor & Francis Web site at
http://www.taylorandfrancis.com

and the CRC Press Web site at
http://www.crcpress.com

Contents

Preface

If you've picked up this book, it's because you have an itch. You've toyed with the idea of being your own boss, running your own professional services consulting firm. Maybe you've dreamed of building a company from nothing, to something with size and value. And maybe you wonder whether this valuable asset can be sold, and for how much.

If you're like many people with this itch, no one has taught you how to build your own firm and to sell it successfully. The task seems daunting, reserved for those people referred to as "entrepreneurs," for which there seems no prescribed course at institutions of higher learning.

While the highway of consulting entrepreneurism is littered with mishaps, many who try to successfully grow their firms do so with stunning results. How do they do it? Do you need special training? Is it rare genius?

The answer, in my opinion, is that you do not need special training, and it's far from genius. But you do need some knowledge, some idea of the do's and don'ts, a liberal dollop of hard work, and a clear strategy. And yes, like all things in life, a little bit of luck helps, but you can make your own luck, too.

And what about you? I have assumed that before you begin this challenge you are, in your own right, a capable consultant—either with aptitude, or with experience. There are many useful books on how to win clients and write successful proposals; I have not tried to replicate these, and I encourage you to refer to them if you are starting consulting. I have not covered legal and indemnity issues, because I have assumed you will research these things before you start your own enterprise.

Instead I have focused on growing an enterprise, creating value in it, and selling it—an approach, a philosophy, and some essential detail. I have tried to distill this into nine chapters, each dealing with a key principle. To broaden the perspective of these lessons, I have included the thoughts and observations of other successful, and not-so-successful, consulting entrepreneurs.

This book contains a growth model that is not out of a textbook, nor out of conventional practice. I developed it as a proprietary model while doing my MBA thesis, and then applied it in real life over the next decade.

I personally credit it with much of the commercial success I have experienced, but I realize that it is not common wisdom. Please use it—with my blessing—with that in mind.

I hope this book, and the lessons offered, help you fulfill your own dreams of growing and selling a successful consulting firm.

Acknowledgments

Ninety percent of what I know about successful consulting enterprises I learned from others over three decades. I have borrowed liberally from their wisdom, actions, and experiences, because many of their stories are more remarkable than my own. Some were successful; others were not. There are valuable lessons in success, and essential lessons in failure.

And while it would be impractical to catalog all who have contributed in some way to this book, the lessons I take from Paul Mitchell, Professor Michael Porter, Terence Jeyaretnam, Errol Briese, Serena Russo, Randal Hinz, Peter Hansen, John Alexander, Sandy Vigar, Graeme Beissel, David Shirley, Chandran Nair, Peter Ryan, Paul Gilding, and Bob McCotter have been particularly insightful.

Victoria Jay and Toni Jordan inspired me to write down my thoughts and experiences, and to share my knowledge. They gave me the benefit of their honesty and wisdom with their tireless reviews. My father Aloysius insisted I write, and for several decades provided an example for me to follow. And my mother Jasmine taught me words, fed me books, and showed me how to like them very much.

An army of clients, too many to recall, taught me (sometimes painfully!) how to be successful at consulting. A smaller legion of staff, in several countries, taught me much, much more, and helped me achieve my own visions. I hope they, too, gained something from their time with me. This book is dedicated to them.

Author

Dr. Raj Aseervatham has more than 30 years' experience in government, private industry, and consulting. He has worked across a broad range of sectors in the United States, South America, Europe, Asia, and Africa. He earned four degrees, including a PhD in engineering, and an MBA majoring in international projects.

In his consulting career, he has established multinational consulting sectors for one of the world's largest consulting firms, started and grown three successful consulting enterprises, and provided strategic direction and governance on the boards of various organizations. His first consulting enterprise had humble beginnings, comprising a laptop in a coffee shop. It grew to strategic consulting for Fortune 500 companies in offices across four continents within 5 years, while he was still in his thirties.

Dr. Aseervatham is passionate about the role of business in improving society's outlook, and continues to work in this area.

1

Lucrative Wisdom

In those days he was wiser than he is now.
He used to frequently take my advice.

Winston Churchill

CORE OF CONSULTING

Let us start with some common knowledge about earnings. Successful consultants do well for themselves.

A qualification—the average consultant is not a multimillionaire. The average consultant merges seamlessly into middle class financial stability. He or she is respectably nondescript, with solid prospects.

Now, the typical *good* consultant is what you might call comfortably well off. He or she is almost certainly financially better off than the average government employee and is likely to be financially better off or at least on a par with successful colleagues in private industry or a corporation. But on the other side of the ledger, any consultant forgoes the relative safety of a fixed salary every month with the more lucrative, but riskier, finances of a hand-to-mouth existence.

Consultants swing from famine to feast in a matter of weeks, while those in government or the corporate world rarely encounter famine. Consulting is to stable household cash flow what Delilah was to Samson. Or what YouTube was to music DVD sales. Somewhat disruptive. But it's the premium that clients pay for intermittent advice (a consultant's hourly fees are typically three to six times an equivalent salary cost for a permanent staff member at the same level) that makes consulting, at its very core, potentially very lucrative. If you can manage the risk of not being hired.

If the average *good* consultant's lot is not so bad—and in the eyes of some, it's actually pretty attractive—then what is in store for the truly successful consultant? The answer is quite a bit. It's not an easy industry and it is cutthroat competitive, but it can be lucrative.

Let's talk numbers to put this in perspective; otherwise it's a philosophical, rather than a practical, exercise. Numbers, as this book will emphasize repeatedly, are important. Numbers reveal truths and debunk myths. When you run a business, look at the numbers to tell you what is possible, probable, and improbable; and listen to the numbers to tell you how you're performing.

Let's talk about "million-dollar consulting." It sounds attractive. You are independent—your own boss—and you earn a million dollars per year. What's not to like? So let's first test the paradigm of the "million-dollar consultant." Let us look at a top-notch consultant, a professional with a very good reputation, who works every day of the year, except for weekends. Let us assume that this very talented and hardworking consultant takes no vacations. He or she works 10 hours a day (100% of which can be billed to the client) and is able to charge $400 for every hour of his/her time; a midrange price.

What we have just described is, of course, full-time employment at 8 hours per day at a good hourly rate, plus paid overtime of 2 hours per day, every day for a year, with no vacations. Not many consultants can claim to be so popular, or so dedicated, but let us stick with it. So this person works 250 days per year, 10 hours per day (or 2500 hours per year) at $400 per hour ... which, if you do the math, is *voila*—a million dollars.

So it is, indeed, possible. But how practical is it? Let us think about it. Where does this type of million-dollar consultant find the time to market to new clients? Maybe the weekends? Will every client pay $400 per hour? Or, put another way, is the type of consulting that our consultant practices worth $400 per hour to all his or her clients? What if you are a human resources consultant and you specialize in developing corporate talent? Or if you are an IT consultant specializing in office networks? Are these necessarily $400-per-hour activities? And what about work/life balance, if you do happen to make the magic million-dollar equation? Can you sustain that work intensity without a vacation indefinitely? How much of this million dollars is paid to the taxman? These are a lot of questions, and the answers are sobering. The term "million-dollar consultant" doesn't quite roll off the tongue now, does it?

Of course, this consultant could earn the million dollars per year without necessarily using an hourly-rate model. One possibility is that the consultant offers a risk-reward contract. "I'll save you a hundred million dollars in operating costs, and my fee is 1% of what I save you." That's a million dollar fee. This is, of course, a good model, but in truth it rarely appears in practice. You are limited to consulting to clients—and in client processes—that have inherent multimillion dollar savings to be had, or inherent multimillion dollar gains to be had. What if you are a humble accountant who is talented in piecing together company accounts for medium-sized enterprises? Or, what if you are an engineer who specializes in designing road infrastructure? Will these multimillion dollar risk/reward opportunities come by often? It's unlikely that they would.

So the million-dollar consultant, while theoretically possible, is not—in a practical sense—probable. It's unlikely you can do it sustainably by yourself because you, the lone consultant, have physical limitations.

Now it is more probable that you can become a sustainable million-dollar consultant if you have people working for you. Most people value financial security and the comfort of a dependable income every month, or every fortnight, or every week. You might pay people their dependable salary, and charge them out as consultants. In other words, you take the cash flow risk of funding permanent salaries and hire them out on a casual consulting basis at higher rates. And, as we established before, most clients will pay three to six times the hourly wage that you pay your staff, for the relative comfort of having your people "on call."

What we have just described is a consulting enterprise. The purpose of this book is to show you how to create this enterprise, to grow it, and eventually to sell it. Why would you sell it? There are two reasons. One, at some point you may decide that the fulfillment of being the boss of your own consulting enterprise is outweighed by the hard work it takes to be continually successful. And two, you may have an asset worth selling. You may choose to exercise the option of capitalizing your wealth and moving on to the next phase of your life. But we will dwell more on that later.

The beauty of creating a successful consulting enterprise (which I will define as a firm with people, a structure, and a market presence), as distinct from being a successful consultant, is that it can be a phenomenally successful activity. Your enterprise will certainly have more capacity for earning than you would, by your lonesome self. It will certainly have more flexibility to provide services to the market. You can take vacations or indulge in the luxury of lying in bed with the flu, and it will keep earning revenue. Your enterprise has the potential to create brand value in ways that you, the individual, may not have. And it has the potential to become much, much bigger than you—until you are just a small cog in its machinery.

"Million-dollar consulting" becomes an everyday term when you have an enterprise, simply because of the scale that is created. It takes, on average, three to four staff to become a million-dollar-per-year consulting enterprise, in today's dollar. Put that way, it's not a very high bar to achieve. Of course, a small firm of three to four staff is unlikely to give you, the owner, a million dollars per year in personal revenue. More scale is required. A profit needs to be created, and dividends need to be payable to you.

Growing an enterprise of scale and value requires hard work. But it's not the classical slog of hard work, the type characterized by mind-numbing repetition with incremental career improvement. It's the hard work of working smart. This type of hard work—this notion of working smart—is no less energy-sapping than its classical counterpart, but it does create its own internal energy within you, the consulting entrepreneur, like a perpetual motion machine. Working smart can be creative and exhilarating. Still, it is hard work—and you, the consulting entrepreneur, cannot shirk the hard work if you want to be successful.

Even a small but successful consulting enterprise accrues value—not just through its profits, but through its clientele and brand. With you at the helm as an owner-operator of a consulting enterprise, the accrued value can translate to early financial independence if the urge takes you there. This can, in turn, allow you to seriously contemplate an early retirement, or a career change, or some other life ambition that you have. And for many people, that's the most attractive part of this journey: the destination, the worlds that it opens up for you *after* you grow your consulting enterprise.

And so be confident that consulting is a bankable industry, if you choose to bank on it. But—be warned—consulting has a feast-to-famine dynamic. It is more reliant on broad economic activity than most other industries. Consultancies prosper in economic growth periods and struggle in times of economic uncertainty and downturns. Of course, the same can be said for almost any industry, but consulting feels the highs and the lows more acutely than most, because it is entirely reliant on the prosperity of clients, and their strategies in the face of the challenges of their markets. There are, of course, exceptions. Some consultancies thrive in bad economic times. Corporate redundancies may result in greater outsourcing than before. Corporate failures create consulting assignments for accountants and lawyers, as well as business consultants hired by others to sell distressed companies. But in general, consulting follows the good times and the bad times of the market.

At the same time, note some characteristics of the consulting industry. Be aware that it is hard to find many mega-consulting firms (compared to other industries) with commensurate multibillion dollar market caps. Ask yourself why that is, and the question is best contemplated through the eyes of an investor. Would you invest in shares in a large consulting company, or would you look at a large bank, or utility, or manufacturing company instead? The answer is usually the latter group of investments. The reason, buried deep, is probably risk. Consulting enterprises carry more risk, for a number of reasons, than other enterprises. And that is partly because the value provided by consulting enterprises to its customers is less concrete than say banks (financial security and returns), utilities (water or power), or manufacturing (a widget). But it is also because of the high dependency on other sectors (its client sectors), the relatively loose regulatory framework on quality that applies to consulting value compared with other sectors and their products, and the proliferation of poor quality consulting, which in turn depreciates the consulting industry's value. There are many more factors that contribute to this risk. But despite its low presence in the share markets, consulting is bankable if you manage your risk factors.

So, while this makes the consulting industry a slightly unsettling investment prospect in your standard stock exchange, it is actually fertile ground for entrepreneurs. Entrepreneurs make the most of higher-risk, higher-reward ventures by managing risk and leveraging the upside. Let us for a moment think like an entrepreneur and consider what consulting is about.

The art of giving advice is alive and well, and it's not likely to die anytime soon. In fact, as the world increases in complexity, the art of advice is likely to thrive. Globalization creates new challenges, which in turn breeds new forms of advice to deal with these challenges. The post–industrial era, the electronic age, post–global financial crisis (GFC) governance, and the increasingly bewildering array of information and misinformation around make sound business advice more valuable than ever before. I use the term "business advice" not to only include "business management consulting" but to broadly encompass consulting about everything to do with running any kind of commercial or governmental activity, such as engineering, logistics, environmental, economics, human resources, strategy, tactical execution, change management, safety ... the list is very long.

The trouble with advice is: there is a lot of it around. Some of it is unsolicited, and you can find this advice almost anywhere—from mothers-in-law, to passengers on airplanes, to taxi drivers, to almost anyone with an opinion. Of course, not all of it is sound, and most readers might agree that mothers-in-law are a case in point (I apologize for this stereotyping; I have only ever had one of them, but I hear rumors).

Some of this plentiful advice is available on the Internet, that world-changing platform of informed, uninformed, misinformed, and partially informed opinion. Free advice is one of the most available commodities in the world. With a bit of a discerning eye, it's fairly easy to mold old, free advice and rebrand it into new and much more expensive advice. Try it. Ask yourself for advice on something you don't know; for example, a strategy to increase productivity in a manufacturing plant or the conservation of marine vegetation in a dredging operation. With a little bit of direction, you should be able to distill a few hours of Internet research work into a summary advisory document. Ask your above-average high school student how to do this, because students today turn out some inspired rehashing of existing knowledge. It is not that hard to provide advice drawn from a highly accessible dumping ground of good and bad information. *What do you call someone who tells you what you already know, then sends you a bill? A consultant.*

In the information age, the barriers to entry for consultants have dropped tremendously. Today—and very likely tomorrow—you don't necessarily have to be an expert at what you do in order to be a paid consultant. You simply need to know more than your client, or have more time to undertake a task than your client does. Access to information is a great leveler in this game. At the same time, the need for consultants has increased, courtesy of the previously mentioned globalization and the deeper connectedness of business decisions with the rest of the world. This has led to a kind of commoditization and deregulation of consulting, and the increased growth of an industry. But with this boom, we also see failed consulting enterprises littering the landscape of advisory services. The sustainable consulting enterprise is a beast that is fast becoming a minority in this industry, while unsustainable consulting 2-year-wannabes scurry around the post-GFC landscape with their short half-lives and even shorter attention spans. Don't be one of those.

If you look around, in government and in private industry, you will find many professionals who, at some point in their careers, turned their hand to consulting. Why did they not stay there? Ask, and you will hear many reasons.

You will hear that consulting is a high-octane industry, and people burn out.

You will hear that the consulting industry is full of shysters and scammers, and many people feel uncomfortable in belonging to that group.

Sometimes you will hear that consulting is like belonging nowhere, too transitory, almost nomadic in existence; and many people like to belong somewhere.

Often you will hear that consulting was taken up out of necessity; perhaps after a person was made redundant. It was not a vocation of choice, just a temporary activity while that person searched for a "real job."

You will almost certainly hear that consulting is intensely competitive.

You will hear many more reasons, and it is important to remember that they reflect the lived experiences of real people, and that they are therefore probably very real.

Do not dismiss them.

So, how will you stay in consulting long enough to build and sell a successful consulting firm? How will your staff stay long enough for you to finish building what you started?

There are many excellent books on consulting. The fundamentals of consulting are well-known, and the skills and knowledge you need to become a good consultant are at your fingertips. But being a consultant and building a strong consulting firm are two entirely different skill sets. You certainly need the first to even contemplate the second. But the second set of skills—those required to build a stable firm—is considerably different, and much more complex.

When I started my first consulting firm, I searched exhaustively for resources that would help to guide my way. I had so many burning questions that my lists of queries spawned their own sublists, like a plague of rabbits with question marks on their quivering fur. Some of the answers were, of course, available in business books and resources. Some of the answers lay in books about consulting. Yet other answers were discovered in books on branding, on innovation, on marketing, on research, and even one on manufacturing. In the end, I found out more than I ever wanted to know, and simultaneously failed to find out about some things that I needed to know. I had to grapple with these latter things myself, some years into my first attempt at creating a consulting enterprise, before I learned them. I had to ask others in my position—other entrepreneurs who were making their own successful consulting firms—how they were addressing the challenges that I could see ahead.

There is no magic formula, but the few most important things to know are important no matter what consulting firm you are trying to grow. These things are easy to understand and, like so many things in this world, much harder to practice because they require diligence, discipline, and leadership. They require sustained effort.

If you enter consulting to make a quick dollar, or to supplement or bridge your personal income, this book won't offer you much. If, on the other hand, you are hoping to create a sustainable business enterprise that accumulates value—value that you can capitalize on—you should read on.

Lessons about consulting come from many perspectives. If you have worked in government or in the private nonconsulting sector, you may have used consultants. The insights to consulting that can be gained from the government and private sector perspectives are useful client perspectives. How are consultants chosen? What are the objective and subjective criteria by which decisions are made? What constitutes a competitive edge from a client perspective? If you have these perspectives, explore them before you start a consulting enterprise. If you do not have these perspectives, talk to government and private sector colleagues who hire consultants.

If you have worked in consulting, you have an advantage in starting your own firm. You may have worked in a small- to medium-sized consultancy, in which you saw in detail how successes and failures are made. You may have worked in a larger consultancy, perhaps further removed from the parts of the organization that could see which strategies delivered profits and growth, but you gained perspectives on market presence, quality control, client segmentation, and so on.

Consulting, however, is not for everyone. It is a constant cycle of pitch and performance; you must promise the client the world in order to win an assignment, and then you must deliver it. The market is, however, surprisingly forgiving, which is why there are many mediocre consulting firms that survive and prosper for a very long time.

One of my colleagues is a university professor who, once upon a time, was a respected consultant in finance and economics. He ran his own firm for a few years, sold it and went into academia. I asked Colin if he ever regretted not maintaining his consulting practice and skills. Did he "settle" too early?

"I was never consulting material," he told me. I was astonished. From what I knew of Colin, and what I had seen, I'd always thought of him as the quintessential consultant. A problem-solver extraordinaire, his career was peppered with country-scale consulting to the World Bank, the International Finance Corporation and others.

"I can see you need an explanation," he observed, grinning. "I found consulting to be—frankly—seedy."

I gasped. Then looked offended. He continued, insensitively,

"Quality gets compromised for the billable hour. It's cutthroat. Half the time you are competing on price. Which impacts on quality. You profess to know the answer when in fact you only have a sense of how to get the answer and a determination to cut-and-paste from other answers. It just felt like smoke and mirrors. After a while, it wasn't for me."

I protested. Colin's work had been groundbreaking, and was still being referred to almost 15 years later when devising country economic policies. Surely he's disproved his point right there?

"I found the majority of consulting to be low level junk, price competitive and value-compromised," he said. "Once in a while we'd get assignments that were unique, and we built our reputation on them, but most of what we did was mundane." He paused, and then made what I thought was his most important point. "But maybe that was because we didn't get our niche right."

Colin was right. Your niche is your key to quality. Beware the consultants who say they know everything, about everything. They are the masters of Google searches and Wikipedia. Their knowledge and insight are limited, in most areas, to what's available in the public domain. That knowledge is not worth paying high consulting rates for. Consequently, if you are not clear on your niche, or niches, you end up competing in circles you have no business being in. You get caught up in low-level consulting, and your differentiator (to nondiscerning clients) becomes price. That model sets a very poor foundation for growth, brand differentiation, and success.

Niche is important.

THREE FORMS OF CONSULTING

Consulting, at its core, is the application of an informed opinion. You're handing out advice. What makes your advice valuable in creating value for the client is what outcomes it generates. When a client seeks advice, the problem presents in one of two forms. One form is the problem that has been encountered by others before, and is therefore not unique. It may have some unique applications in the client context, but it is largely not a unique problem. The other form is the opposite—a unique problem for which there is no preexisting solution that you can cut, paste, and adapt. The most valuable piece of consulting is called for when there is a problem, and the solution is not evident. If the problem is big enough and important enough to solve, it clearly commands a high price. When a solution is delivered, the successful consultant earns both a fee and a reputation for solving a unique and complex problem. When the next similar complex problem comes along, that successful consultant has accrued a differentiator in the market.

Let us look at a simple relationship for successful problem solving. The relationship is important because it contains the ingredients for highly successful consulting enterprises.

Successful problem solving requires knowledge + analysis + insight

Let us start with the simplest assumption. You have knowledge that the client can use. This may be as simple as knowing how to do something that is not particularly rare or unique, but it is useful. It may include experience, which is simply the repeated and effective application of knowledge. Being knowledgeably informed does not mean you are a walking encyclopedia. Although being a walking encyclopedia never hurts, not many people can genuinely claim that they are one of those. Even the masters of Internet research. But in order to solve a problem, you need some knowledge.

Analysis allows you to use knowledge wisely. In problem solving, you are trying to figure out why the problem exists or why the problem might exist in the future, and then you are trying to work out how to make it cease to exist. So, knowledge plus analysis gives you an informed opinion.

Your informed opinion is not as bland as the average point of view. Everyone has a point of view, and clients are unlikely to pay much for a point of view. That is, unless there is something special about it; something extra, perhaps like the depth of analysis you bring. People may not even listen to your opinion, for free, at parties, unless you have this something extra. This analysis makes your knowledge more potent than the mere assimilation of information and know-how.

And finally, your problem solving is brought to life with insight. Insight is the difference between a problem solved theoretically, and a problem solved in practice, both effectively and efficiently. It is the application of an informed opinion to a set of circumstances that is in some way unique. Each client setting is different, and therefore the application of informed opinion is different in each setting. Your informed opinion might work with client A and client B, but your insights might lead to a different implementation for the two clients, resulting in a bespoke and higher-value outcome for each client. Insights are relevant when you take account of client cultures, of specific operational circumstances, external factors, and so on that have a bearing on how potent your informed opinion might be.

All of which brings us to the three basic forms of consulting. Each form of consulting activity has a different value to a client, and therefore a different value to you, the consultant. Going back to basics, value to you can be broken down into two things—the unit value (which is the consulting proposition's value-per-hour) and the volume of the consulting proposition (which is the number of person-hours the client pays for). Depending on your point of view, and your consulting strategy, it might be more valuable to you to access low-volume-high-value-per-hour consulting or high-volume-low-value-per-hour consulting or something in between. There is no right answer, but being clear on which of the three basic forms of consulting you focus on or what proportions of each you focus on is important to your strategy and to your success. Ultimately though, consulting is simply the client's decision to bring in someone from outside to undertake a task. It is worth keeping that humble view in mind, while recognizing the three types of motivation that propel a client to hire a consultant.

Broadly, the three types of consulting available to you are *body shopping*, *knowledge-based consulting,* and *value-based consulting.* They are listed in order of increasing complexity, and each can be more successful than the other depending on the supply and demand circumstances that your firm is operating within.

There is no clear winner, and it is important you choose carefully to suit your personal and professional circumstances, the market conditions where you are, and your strategy.

Body Shopping

Body shopping is the art of finding the right people, in the right quantity, with the right skills, to undertake a task. It is largely a resourcing issue.

In body shopping, the client hires a consultant to do a task that he or she cannot do because of time or resource pressures. The client (either the individual or the organization) is quite capable of undertaking the task, but for one reason or another, it is not near the top of their personal to-do list. A client resorts to body shopping when deadlines are tight or there are not enough people to undertake the task in the time available; or the task is commoditized in some way (for example the tasks are a "lower-level" task for your organization); or human resource (for example "headcount") constraints force you to outsource a task.

Let us use a simple analogy, which we will apply for each type of consulting. You hire a gardener to prune your hedges, although you know that it is something you could probably do if you were so inclined and had the time. You have just made a body-shopping transaction. Note, this does not mean that you could prune your hedges as well as a professional gardener could, but you could undertake a passable job if you had to. As you would imagine, body shopping is generally not top-dollar consulting in terms of the unit rate that clients will pay, unless time pressures are extreme and/ or the task is critical.

Globalization did interesting things to the body-shopping proposition. It brought scale to the prospect, and it made it more attractive. It made it much easier to access, from outside of a client organization, commoditized, and noncore, skills. As a result of easier access, the available pool of body-shopping resources expanded dramatically. Witness the birth, rise, and continued rise of outsourced services such as call centers and IT service providers. The activity morphed in scale from a simple consulting proposition to a large-scale contracting proposition. The consulting propositions discussed in this book are not of this extreme variety; we will confine comments to more modest and much smaller-scale body-shopping concepts.

David worked for a while in the building industry as a carpenter, before deciding on formal education, in this case engineering. When he entered University, he was quite a bit older than his peers. During the longer semester breaks, he would hire a group of contractors and build a house for a client. He did it quickly and efficiently, and took care of all the details and project management that his clients wanted to avoid.

By the time David graduated, he was completely disinterested in finding a job. While the rest of his graduating class competed ferociously in the job market, David got himself a loan and continued his building enterprise. He hired people like himself who would build houses—they could hire the right tradespeople, manage the procurement and delivery of materials; all of the menial details that clients preferred not to concern themselves with. He expanded, from housing, to local Council developments, to roads, rail and infrastructure.

He never looked back, building a strong firm whose base of income was derived from body-shopping. In other words, doing what the client could not be bothered doing (or could not justify the fixed cost of carrying the requisite people to do the work), and hiring lots of people to get the work done. He only made a small percentage profit on each person he hired, but he hired a lot of people. And so, like the millionaire who became rich by selling one-dollar gadgets, he created success from the bulk selling of people-hours. He offered little that was special or unique other than exemplary professionalism, but he filled a void in the market that asked for a high volume of this commodity.

David's model pivots around a single consultant (a project manager for a building project) who leverages this position with a much bigger body-shopping concept. His clients, who are railway companies, road and transport authorities, and local councils, have the ability to undertake this work. However, it is worth more to them if they do not invest in the fixed costs of carrying the required people; and so they downsize and elect to bring in companies like David's to do the work as and when required. David caters for this labor-shift concept.

David reflects that "The model is scalable, both up and down. In bad times I can shrink easily, and in good times I can expand very quickly to meet market needs. Every so often government departments move to out-sourcing models, and this gives me the momentum to grow in reasonably large steps."

Knowledge-Based Consulting

The second form of consulting can be thought of as *knowledge-based* consulting. This form of consulting accesses unique knowledge or skills that the consultant may possess. This is a more rare commodity in the market for the client to access. Consequently, the client may not have the potential to hold the skills in-house (and may never want to, especially if the knowledge or skill is only applied sporadically or in challenging circumstances). This form of consulting commands a premium. This premium increases with the rarity of the knowledge or skill being applied, and the value it unleashes for the client.

The beauty of knowledge-based consulting is that it seems to be a perpetual-motion machine. The more complex our world gets, the more the world of niche, knowledge-based consulting expands. And the more niche, knowledge-based activities are propagated, the more complex our world gets. It's an ever-expanding circle of knowledge and complexity.

A new gas economy sees us creating lower-carbon fuels and exporting them into markets to feed growing energy demands and an increasing reluctance to exploit higher-carbon fossil fuels. In this evolving fuel economy, knowledge-based innovations make the fuel transfer proposition more efficient, more productive, and more adaptive to growing energy economies. This in turn helps to propagate a more vibrant and diverse gas economy, which creates more need for innovative efficiencies and differentiators, and so on. Complexity never dies. Knowledge-based consultants have a bright future, provided they understand the need to redefine and renew the boundaries of rare knowledge.

Continuing with the metaphor of the gardener that you might hire, we can think of an example of knowledge-based consulting. You might need specialist knowledge in picking the trees and shrubs, the potting mixes and irrigation systems that are best suited to the climate and soils around your house. The key purchase here is knowledge, which you do not currently hold in-house, and which would require considerable investment on your part to acquire.

> Chris and Kelly were a brother-and-sister team in the year above mine who, with their twin First-Class-Honors degrees, landed scholarships to do their PhDs. In a stroke of genius—which probably justified their First Class Honors results more convincingly than their academic colors—they earned PhDs in related areas. This effectively meant that they harnessed not one, but two knowledge-based disciplines, and joined them together. Four years later, they opened up a niche consulting firm—an arcane area of high strength steel in bridges and virtuoso architectural buildings. There was virtually no competition, at least in a 2000-mile radius. The firm grew tremendously quickly and was engaged on a number of prestigious projects.
>
> Their challenge, which is not uncommon in knowledge-based consulting, is that they were short of understudies to capitalize on this niche market. In other words, growth in that niche market was hampered by the lack of people with their rarified knowledge. Chris and Kelly had no significant mentoring program to speak of, to create clones of themselves. So while they commanded high consulting fees for themselves, there was limited leverage. Meanwhile, other, larger consulting firms—recognizing the successful market penetration the siblings had achieved—began creating their own skill sets in this area. The market became more competitive. Chris and Kelly had a market advantage in that they were recognized as being the most experienced in the field, but they were losing market share and their company had stagnated.

Knowledge-based consulting is probably the most widely applied form of consulting in the industry. There are many niches to explore, even within relatively specific areas of expertise such as business, engineering, science, public relations, law, security, and others; which means that the market is diverse. Chris and Kelly's model of knowledge-based consulting capitalized on a high-value, high-demand, and rare niche activity.

Free markets, unfortunately, don't allow rarity and demand to coexist for very long. Competition sets in, and rarity is eroded in a relatively short period of time. However, during that period where your firm possesses rare skills that are in demand, you can command high fees. It is important to acknowledge that rare knowledge is not a permanent asset, and ensure that your consulting firm either commands a strong monopoly on the knowledge-based service that is provided, continues to create knew knowledge frontiers in that area of expertise, or diversifies into other knowledge-based activities. A static niche is a dangerous niche.

Value-Based Consulting

The third form of consulting is *value-based* consulting. In value-based consulting, insight is dialed up in problem-solving acumen. To deliberately use the word "value" in a circular proposition, the value of value-based consulting depends on the organizational value that the solved problem brings to the client organization. If a client organization wants to, say, transform its supply chain efficiency, and the savings the transformation brings is $1 million per year for many years to come, the consultancy is worth around $2 million (if you believe, as many would, that a 2-year return on investment is attractive).

Value-based consulting is not as easy to grow as the other two genres. It occupies a relatively small space in the consulting world. You might incorrectly assume that knowledge-based consulting would be the smaller niche because specialist knowledge is uncommon. But the reality is otherwise. Value-based consulting is applied to more unique problems, which by definition are rare. After all, if the same problem had been solved a few times before, the ability to solve the problem again has probably become a knowledge-based consultancy proposition. Value-based consulting requires thought leadership and innovation, and innovation is a one-off proposition.

The gardener you hired in this example might be expected to design the garden around your house so that it has the appropriate feng shui, the mix of landscape elements that imparts a certain character that you favor, synergy with the design of the house and the potential to add considerably to the resale value of the property. For another property, which might have different slopes and soils and a completely different architectural layout to the building, there is a different unique value proposition.

Most consulting firms claim to "add value" and most claim innovative abilities. This is because, in the world of consulting, value-based outcomes are prized. For the consultant, it has considerable reputational value and, among consultants, it is a class differentiator. First class consulting has value-based outcomes, second-class consulting is something anyone can do. Many consultants aspire to the value-based brand.

The client rewards you not for the hours worked, but for the outcome produced (although you will still be expected to account for the hours worked!). But what hourly rate do you place on genius? Does it matter if it only took me 3 days to produce a masterpiece of consulting that will transform your organization and net you a million dollars? Would you pay $50,000 for that piece of genius, or in excess of $15,000 a day for that demonstrable value? Most clients would.

> An early consulting mentor with an offbeat sense of humor once gave me an invaluable piece of advice. On a long flight and three wines into the meal service I was (dangerously, given that he was my boss's boss), confessing that my vision was not to work for a consulting firm, but to run my own firm. He said, "Let me give you some advice then. For every five hard-working consultants you hire, make sure you have at least one who's inherently lazy. Lazy, but not afraid of hard work, that's important, you understand? That kind of consultant is always, ALWAYS, searching for an easier way to do their job, an easier way to do everything. When they find value, they REALLY find value."
>
> I was enthralled. He had just made a virtue of the one characteristic that my high school teachers had nagged me about for years on end.
>
> "But don't let that be YOU on this assignment," he finished with a dry chuckle.

This mentor was, of course, talking about innovation. His five-to-one ratio of hardworking consultants to innovative consultants was not dissimilar to my experiences in real life. The innovative shortcut or the unique solution to a problem occurs much less often than the knowledge-based solution because it is often impractical or inefficient to "reinvent the wheel." Many existing solutions are adaptable to variations of the same problem or even different problems. However, where there is a newer and better way of doing something or a solution for a previously unsolved problem, there is tremendous value. Value-based consulting recognizes this value and pursues it.

YOUR SHELF LIFE

So, on the sliding scale of consultancy value, body shopping is worth less (per unit of effort) than knowledge-based consulting, which in turn is worth less (per unit of effort) than value-based consulting. Obviously, this is not a hard-and-fast rule; for example, a body-shopping assignment on a critical deadline might be worth more to a client than a more leisurely knowledge-based assignment. And of course, consulting assignments can be hybrids of two or more of the three forms of consultancy outlined.

Why is your understanding of the forms of consultancy important in creating your own enterprise? Other than the obvious (they help define the "charge out rate" or revenue base of a consultancy), they also impact heavily on how you shape your offering in the market, how you recruit into your firm, and how you remunerate and reward your staff.

But much of consulting has a short shelf life. The higher-value end of consulting is, much like a bright star that burns out quickly, often of fleeting value. This is because we live in an age of information, where knowledge continues to expand at an astonishing rate and the increasing complexity of the world requires greater insights to be successful. This is not a bad thing, because it means high-value consulting regenerates itself through knowledge and innovation. The solution that worked yesterday may not work as well today or tomorrow. And this means more work, more analysis, and insight are required to deliver value. But it also means the competitive edge is fierce, and staying on top of your game is essential. At the lower-value end of consulting, the pace is less frenetic and the pressure to analyze and generate insights is much less. At the higher end, the stakes are greater because not every complex problem tackled results in an acceptable solution.

These days, in a corporation, many leadership programs are built around the concept of comfort with ambiguity. Great value is placed on being able to set clear direction with a clear "why" even if the data you have is fuzzy, the future is in flux and all of the moving parts of your decision points are rotating at once. This ambiguous universe is where some of the highest value consulting propositions exist, but perhaps where the greatest enterprise risks also lie.

Gordon, a CEO of a multinational company spoke at a consulting innovation conference where he claimed that he had met many consultants who, surprisingly to him, abhorred ambiguity.

"The consulting life, at face value, doesn't offer long-term outlooks. How long does your cash flow projection last? Three months? Mine lasts several years. Your contracts are a few months on average. Mine are five to ten year supply contracts. Consulting careers are inherently uncertain. So why then are many consultants so uncomfortable with uncertainty?"

A conference attendee in the crowd asked him what made him think that consultants were uncomfortable with uncertainty.

"My experience is that far too many consultants take solutions from one problem and try to apply it to another. Maybe that's one way to achieve efficiency, but I wonder if they have taken on the project BECAUSE they already have a pre-delivered solution in mind. Consultants will willingly work on an hourly rate for no fixed scope, but are wary of starting fixed-price contracts unless the problem and outcome are clear. And when I suggest a risk-reward contract, they almost run out the door in panic!"

Uncomfortable as it was for many consultants in the room to hear, it seemed he had a point. Consulting organizations are populated by individuals who are perfectly happy to propose a solution for their clients, and then send them a bill. They don't have to live with the outcome themselves. Are there many consultants who take risk/reward contracts? These are contracts where, for example, you work for a minimum retainer but if your solution works, you get paid a proportion of the upside. In essence, the base pay is low or modest, with the potential of very high pay if the job is done well. The answer appears to be no; most consultants consider this to be a disadvantageous model for them. Yet truly innovative consultants could do very well in this area.

THE CONSULTANT'S WORLD

There is an element of the consultant's genre that is not discussed much, and yet there is a great deal of insight in it, particularly, if you are building your own firm. It has to do with the consultant's place in the professional world, and the subculture that forms around this place.

Consultants are like gunslingers for hire. If you have a problem, you bring one in. You don't want them around for long, because they are expensive. And they are not of your kind. They do not belong in your firm.

Their culture is not yours. Just like the gunslinger who doesn't belong in your town, you want to see them gone when the job is done. In Japan, they are *ronin*, masterless samurai, people of ambiguous loyalties. They are, to be sure, potent and talented, but there is a vague tragedy about their existence just outside the hub of society.

And despite its glamour, the consultant's life can be professionally unfulfilling. Clients can ask for advice, and they will pay for it, but they don't have to take your advice. A good consultant finds solutions to problems, and some of those solutions are not that popular. If you recommend a client downsizes, or strengthens management to make better decisions, or spends millions of dollars in retrofitting their operation, these are all painful actions. As most gunslingers probably know, the adage is true: you can take a horse to water, but you can't make it drink. As a consultant, you spend a lot of time seeing what *could be*, and then watching— unfulfilled—as it never *is*. Sometimes your advice is taken and sometimes it is not. You learn to move on, never owning the problem or the solution. If you are passionate about your work, which is an asset to any consultant, there can often be a sense of emptiness about some of your work, a sense of futility. Older consultants, like their grizzled gunslinger counterparts, can be deeply cynical. They are too easily able to see faults and too easily able to shrug and walk away without guilt if their advice is not taken. They are too ready to see good intentions undone by inadequate commitment.

Like everything in life, consulting has its own yin and yang. But at its heart, it is a dynamic and lucrative world. It is slightly mysterious, the phrase *I am a consultant* managing to span the breadth of ambiguity between trusted advisor and assassin-for-hire. And its beauty is that anyone who knows something can be a consultant. The barriers to entry into the consulting world are astoundingly low.

Why is this important? In Chapters 3, 4, and 5 we spend time on the culture of the firm that you grow. In consulting, the cultural background has the same common denominator—that gunslinger element—the band of *ronin*, the slight sense of displacement. You only need spend time in a conference, watching people mingling, to see this. The consultant is easy to spot. He or she is constantly on the move, handing out business cards and networking like his or her livelihood depend on it. Which, obviously, it does. Meanwhile the other professionals, from client organizations or government organizations, display an array of body language that tells you that the consultant is an outsider. Even if the consultant is highly respected, his or her place in these professional circles seems slightly awkward. There is a wariness among many of his or her peers, a defensive air against the consulting sales pitch that may or may not happen. There is a guardedness against this person who has no allegiance to a corporation or a government department, who prowls outside those organizations like a wolf from another, unknown, pack.

As you build your firm, empathize with the slight displacement that your staff might experience in the wider professional world. Create a familial culture that compensates for this, creates strong allegiances within your firm and flourishes into a web of loyalty. Build in your firm a sense of professional excellence and intellectual strength that translates to pride in each of your staff. There is a reason that corporations and government departments are populated by people who *used* to be consultants. Many of them experienced their consulting lives as a slightly uncomfortable transit lounge in which they waited for the right flight to the right destination; a destination that offered for them a sense of belonging and purpose. Part of your challenge is to create in your firm a culture that delivers that destination right at their doorstep. That culture will underpin how successfully you grow, and sell, your consulting firm.

THREE TIPS

Tip 1: There are three types of consulting. Be very clear about what type of consulting you want to offer, and—if you choose a hybrid of two or three of these types—how much of each component of the hybrid you have. Be as clear as you can about your choice because it underpins your strategy.

Tip 2: Make sure you are genuinely cut out—personally, emotionally, and professionally—for consulting. Think of the analogy to *ronin* that was made earlier—those masterless samurai. Is that you? No one else, except you, can tell you whether you are. Be sure.

Tip 3: Be good (top 10 percentile good) at something in your field. When you first start, your personal credibility is everything. Clients and employees alike will be drawn to unique and valued skill sets. What are yours?

2

Exit Strategy

If you want a happy ending, that depends, of course, on where you stop your story.

Orson Welles

WRITING YOUR STORY BACKWARD

If you know where you are going, you are more likely to get there.

Your journey will have purpose and motivation if you start with the Exit Strategy. Without a consulting firm yet in place, try to work out how you are going to sell one. Some people find this startling. How do you think about selling something when you don't actually have that something? Others find it a bit dispassionate and abstract. How can you start something when your focus is on finishing? Yet, in reality, this approach is pragmatic, engaging, and purposeful.

Passionate professionals who love their work might feel like this is too calculating, almost heresy. What about the people you hire? Aren't you starting with an abandonment mindset? Shouldn't you wait and see how it goes before forming an Exit Strategy?

These are good questions, but as we proceed you will see that there are even better answers. Throughout this chapter, we identify issues that will affect both the journey to the exit, and the exit itself. Some of these issues are best thought about at the beginning of the enterprise, rather than halfway through or at the end. Planning your company with these issues in mind could very well save you months, years, and a lot of money.

Many people ask if they can start their firm without this Exit Strategy in mind. The answer is yes, of course. It is perfectly reasonable to start a firm and see how everything goes. It is completely feasible to grow a firm without an Exit Strategy, and it is entirely plausible that you can sell that firm without starting with an Exit Strategy. However, this is not a strategy. It is adaptive management, and it is a potentially meandering path. You are much more likely to execute an effective exit from a firm that you start and grow if you plan to do so from the time you start it. You are much more likely to do this quicker. You are much more likely to do this purposefully and make the right decisions along the way to achieve your goal as directly as possible.

As we will explore in this chapter, and in later chapters, your successful Exit Strategy will have nothing to do with abandoning your staff, and everything to do with empowering them. By starting your firm with an Exit Strategy in mind, you will soon ponder the management structure that supports your exit, and this will take you very quickly to developing and mentoring a strong leadership team. There is a risk that you will not focus enough on this people development aspect unless you seriously consider the smooth operation of a company without you there to guide it.

And so, despite all the protests to the contrary that you might hear, the philosophy of starting with the Exit Strategy brings a finite purpose to the enterprise. Nothing focuses the mind as much as a finite purpose, an end for which the means must be created. That is the mindset that you, as the leader of this firm, will benefit most from, if your desire is to grow and sell a successful consulting firm.

What does an Exit Strategy look like? For most of this book, the exit is the point of sale. However, other endgames are valid too, including winding down your company, handing over control to your team and sitting in the background, or just running it until you no longer have the will or energy to do so. Endgames such as listing your company publicly on the stock market, while also valid, are quite rare. They also require strategies of larger scale than this book provides, and so we will not explore that scenario. However, the most purposeful—and challenging—strategy is to exit with the sale of a capital asset. If you can set yourself up for this exit but have a change of heart, all other endgames are relatively easy to implement. The comparison is similar to the marathon runner who prepares by choosing courses that include many challenging hills; this training gives him or her a natural advantage on the easier courses.

Exit Strategies are commonplace in many companies, particularly start-ups. But Exit Strategies in consulting have some unique characteristics. Consulting enterprises are not like retail chains or telecommunications or mining companies, which all trade an interchangeable commodity. Customer service is, of course, important (and can be a key differentiator in some sectors) but the commodity that is being sold can, theoretically, be sold without much people input. In consulting, all of the commodity that is sold is 100% reliant on people input. Therefore the worth of consulting firms lies very much in their people, and the solutions they create and execute.

Let's take a break from working backward for a minute, and work forward from a start-up as a sole consulting operator.

When starting a consulting enterprise, that worth is you, the key person. At that point, you have a personal brand and a small following of clients. You can keep yourself fed with work and you may even frequently be offered more work than you can possibly do while maintaining a healthy work-life balance. But the consulting company at that point is largely you. This means that you control 100% of the commodity that is sold, because you personally generate it. So, maintaining brand value is relatively easy when the only parameter to manage is you.

You may, in time, have one, two, or even a few apprentices. You continue to exert strong influence on the commodity that is sold, and you manage the client relationships. The brand value is still mostly you, but you have managed to increase output capacity.

At some point, you're going to want to retire, and you might not necessarily want the worth of your enterprise to go to pasture with you. Of course, putting your consulting firm to pasture is a viable option, although we do not discuss it in this book. It is not an option that provides a financial maturity outcome, and it may not be the best option for you. If you decide that you do not want to disband what you have and you want to leave a legacy behind, you're faced with the choices about your exit (or an appropriate endgame) that we highlighted earlier.

This fork in the road can occur relatively early in your consulting career or relatively late. It is best to proceed beyond this fork in the road only when your Exit Strategy is firmly developed. Some people might "play it by ear" until they reach this fork, and then contemplate viable Exit Strategies. Others might prefer to think through the Exit Strategy before they begin putting their money into their consulting venture. It all depends on you. Is time an important factor for you? Are you a seasoned consultant, or do you need to get a feel for consulting before deciding whether growing and selling a consulting firm is something you are confident doing?

By now, you should sense that the most efficient way to grow and sell a successful consulting firm is to not start until you have an Exit Strategy. The less efficient way, but possibly more in the comfort zone of some, is to wait until you get to that fork in the road before you devise your Exit Strategy.

But why, of the options available at the fork in the road or before, would some readers want to grow a consulting enterprise and sell a successful, thriving business to a buyer? The reason for most is post-sale independence. Cashing out and moving onto something else is an elegant way to create a step-improvement in financial independence, and create new and exciting options for your life path. It is entrepreneurship at its most fluent and liberating; the start-up and cash-out cycle.

While you might want the entrepreneurship model, others might want to grow a consulting enterprise to see them through a successful career and then a part-time retirement. Whatever your motivation, you need to spend some time on it and clearly define it to yourself. This vision is the backdrop, the horizon, and the driver for the blueprint of your strategy.

As we established earlier, it is much easier to nurse your consulting enterprise into your retirement than to plan to sell it. It's not so much an Exit Strategy as a moving-in strategy, and there is no significant gear change to plan for. You set your cruise control until you run out of fuel. Although many of the insights in this book work well enough for a moving-in strategy, there is a sense of urgency that you will pick up while reading the next few chapters. That sense of urgency assumes you have a defined-target Exit Strategy; in this case, it is the creation of a high-value enterprise that you can leave, in exchange for some capital, in a reasonably short period of time.

If you want to exit at some point and cash out, you need a very well-defined strategy. The more you are inclined to "see how it goes" after that fork in the road, the tougher it will be to execute an Exit Strategy. Early clarity is incredibly important here, or you risk meandering and wasting a lot of time.

And while clarity is a phenomenal asset, the reality is that some of your valiant striving for clarity might not actually ever result in 100% clarity. That's OK, don't sweat it. The key thing is that you search relentlessly for clarity, and know that every morsel you pick up will add up to a greater degree of clarity. More clarity is a good thing. It will crystallize purpose and build confidence. The morsels combine and coalesce until, suddenly, your Exit Strategy starts to manifest into something that you don't just hope for, but you actually believe in. It's like preparing for a high jump in athletics. You visualize the high jump, the run-up, the bar, the mat beyond, the sky above, running over and over in your mind the small details that, together, result in a successful clearing of the bar. With enough visualization and attention to clarity and detail, your mind moves from "I think I can" to "I know I will."

KNOW YOUR EXIT VALUE PERSPECTIVES

When you exit via a sale, there are two very important perspectives to understand and connect. If you don't connect these perspectives, there is no sale. Your perspective, as the seller, is obviously one perspective. The other, and very important perspective, is your buyer's.

Your own perspective will come with both conscious and unconscious bias, and if you do not guard against them, you will find that your exit is a difficult and stressful one. It might even be disappointing. Guard against theses biases throughout the development of your business. These biases stem from one very simple fact—this business is your baby. And, like all parents, you will be predisposed to a generous and complimentary view of your baby. Your successful business will seem like the pinnacle of your achievements, it will be near-perfect, and you will be righteously indignant at any suggestion to the contrary.

Your buyer is likely to be more objective, and tuned in to any miniscule flaw in your business. Your buyer will make decisions based on potential, while your perspective will be based on achievement. While your buyer views every characteristic of your business as a potential indicator for the future, your mindset will be colored by the past. Your valuation of your business will be tempered by the success you have enjoyed, while for your buyer the past is largely irrelevant. It is what is presented today and what it means for the future that is important to the buyer.

Your buyer will negotiate because that is the buyer's job. Why pay $10 million for a company when you can get it for $8 million? Your (seller's) pride may balk at such a thought, but your buyer is thinking about the extra $2 million that can be employed in his or her growth strategy for your business. For the buyer, pride will have no place in the negotiation.

And so, at the point of exit, there is a real risk that you, the seller, are infused with pride and emotion; and that the buyer is intent on getting the best deal possible. If that is the case, you—the seller—are going to find the process of exit more frustrating and stressful than it needs to be. Your objective, then, should be to arrive at the negotiating table with as little emotive perspective as possible. Your objective should be to arrive at that table as a clinical, financial calculating machine. Or as close as possible as you can get to that state.

This means preparing for the point of exit—getting ready for sale—from the very start.

So let us understand how a consulting enterprise might be valued by a buyer, and how you might use that perspective to get the best exit scenario you can. To be honest, without bursting your bubble at this early stage, the buyer's perspective is probably more important than yours!

First, there is an accounting value. In accounting terms, there is a simple and mostly objective equation that determines a possible sale value, which we will call the Quick Enterprise Value Estimate or QEVE.

$$Enterprise\ value = \left(Multiplier \times average\ net\ profit \right) + Assets - Liabilities$$

It is important to understand this equation, because key decisions around your Exit Strategy pivot around what it tells you. Let's break it down, leaving the multiplier to the end.

The average net profit is what your buyer might hope to gain every year as a result of buying your enterprise. Think of it as similar to a price-to-earnings ratio of shares, although we are not working in a share market so the conventional wisdom about acceptable price-to-earnings ratios does not apply here. If the buyer does nothing to your enterprise but continues to manage it as you have done for some years, he or she is entitled to expect that the average profit would stay much the same, all other things being equal.

The buyer's financial perspective is that first and foremost, he or she wants to recoup the money paid for the consulting enterprise in as little time as possible. This is the time it takes to break even. Any buyer wants to reduce capital risk, and the time to pay back expended capital is an important element of capital risk. It is useful, in these scenarios, to think of what that expectation would look like if the buyer did nothing with the business except run it like you have been running it. This gives you a starting point for seeing your buyer's perspective.

If a buyer cannot see a breakeven outcome within 2 or 3 years, a question mark is produced. The question mark will usually form around the sale price. Is it too high? How will the buyer get the sale price low enough so that the time to break even is not 3 years (an uninspiring prospect), possibly 2 years (an interesting prospect) or even 1 year (an exciting prospect)?

The average net profit can be calculated a variety of ways. Using the average of the last 3 years' profit before sale is a reasonable benchmark, if the profit has been relatively stable or has grown somewhat from year to year. If the profit has been a bit of a rollercoaster ride (high one year, low the next, high again the year after) then another question mark is raised about the stability of cost or revenue. If it has dwindled slightly over the 3 years, yet another question mark arises. Is the market softening or are clients slowly moving away—perhaps even as a prelude to a mass exodus? The most comforting trend is a strong and steady year on year rise in profit, which indicates good growth prospects. Even a skyrocketing profit, leaping in spectacular bounds from one year to the next, can raise question marks. Is your profit increase a result of some short-term burst in the market? Is your service offering a fad?

So the average net profit, when peeled back a little bit, may have a story to tell the buyer. It is worth thinking about what you want that story to be—that is, what an appealing story might sound like to a potential buyer—and ensuring that your growth strategy can evidence that story. The average net profit is the foundation of the accounting formula discussed earlier.

Assets are the tangible things that the company holds (cash in the bank, equipment and debtors, for example). For a consulting company—unless you have a lot of cash in the bank, you own the office premises or you have high-capital value equipment—this may not be a significant factor. Consulting firms often make the mistake of overinvesting in assets that add little to sale value. A buyer is unlikely to be overly impressed if you have the fastest network hub money can buy, or the best printer. A decent, functioning asset of this kind will do just fine. Of course, conversely, a buyer might be distinctly unimpressed if your network hub crashes weekly or your printer looks and functions like a reject from an op shop.

Buyers also place very little value premium on your office space—how well it is furbished and how well it is furnished. These accouterments are for the benefit of your staff and clients. Nine out of ten times, a buyer has a different office setup in mind than the one you are proud of. It is not uncommon to hear consulting business owners proudly display a six-figure fit-out and claim that it has increased the value of their business.

It may have increased the amenity of the business to your employees and clients, which is a good thing, but it is not to be confused with a direct uplift in your sale price.

Assets have the disconcerting habit of depreciating. This means that, according to the accountant's valuation in the aforementioned equation, your asset is worth 10%–20% less than what it was a year ago. By the time, you have had an asset for 5 years, it is worth just a shadow of what you paid for it. Some good generic advice on consulting assets is to own as little as possible, except for those assets that either accrue in value or give you a tax advantage. Applied broadly, its practical outcome is that your consulting firm might own precious few physical assets.

Several consultants have benefitted greatly at the point of sale from buying their office premises at the start of their enterprise growth. While any real estate proposition comes with risk, owned office space can be an asset that accrues in value over time, and one for which interest on loan payments may create a tax advantage. When choosing assets, ask your accountant to go through your premises and equipment list and highlight those items that meet his or her definition of assets that might add to the sale value of your business. Prioritize those assets, and think about renting or leasing other assets. Avoid accumulating assets that give you a disappointingly low number in the asset column when you think you have invested a lot of money in creating asset value.

Your list of invoices is a variable asset that factors significantly in your sale. This list shows how many clients owe you money. The list is complex, and tells an important story. For example, if 70% of your invoices are sent to one client, you may be carrying a key client risk. More confidence is created in your list of invoices if the money owed to you is distributed among many clients, with no key client risk elements. This confidence can swing the other way, too. If your list of clients is very long and the money owed to you by each is very small, your enterprise looks like a nickel-and-dime business.

The most comforting invoice list looks like a normal distribution. A normal distribution is sometimes known as nature's distribution. It shows a natural order of things, and it is often appreciated for just being—well—*normal*. Your normal distribution of invoices for a year looks something like Figure 2.1.

At the middle of your normal distribution is your average expected income per client. If the average expected income per client is close to or higher than your average individual salary cost, the quality of your invoice list is considered quite good.

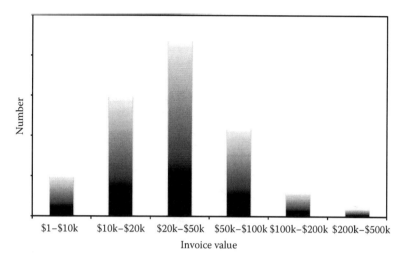

FIGURE 2.1
Normal distribution of invoices.

But not all clients pay invoices, so yet another lens is applied to your invoice list. Your bad debts are the evil shadow of your invoice list. Naturally, you want to aim for zero bad debts, but this might be out of your control. If you are going to have bad debts, it is best to have them represented on the left hand side of your normal distribution. In other words, if you have bad debts and they infrequently appear only with the clients who owe you little money, you have the lowest risk invoice-default story to tell.

But there is more. Peeling away another layer is a story that all buyers are interested in. We will touch on this further when we talk about the very important operational cash flow. This next layer, again applied to your invoice list, is your aged debtors. An aged debtor analysis shows your buyer how long your clients take to pay you. It is useful to bracket this into four timeframes. The first is 0–30 days, which is considered relatively timely payment. The second, 30–60 days, is a bit sluggish and will cause your potential buyer to furrow his or her brow to begin the self-talk that comes before negotiation on price. The third, 60–90 days is, frankly, concerning. The fourth—greater than 90 days—is downright alarming, and probably indicates a predisposition to bad debts.

The healthiest picture you can show is, of course, that 100% of your invoices are paid in less than 30 days. But this, while not impossible, is quite a rare occurrence. A practical and not-too-disconcerting picture might look something like Figure 2.2.

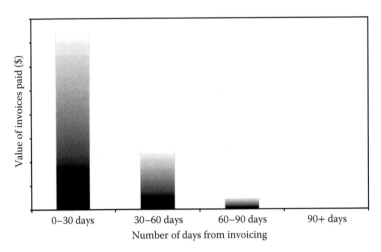

FIGURE 2.2
Typical aged debtors chart.

Liabilities are the opposite of assets. A buyer views all liabilities as a burden that must be carried, and so they are scrutinized very carefully. Loans and creditors (people that you owe money to, such as suppliers) are good examples of liabilities. It is generally impossible to avoid creditors but, as we will discuss later, it is a good idea to think very carefully before borrowing money for your enterprise; and a great idea to avoid loans on your balance sheet at the point of sale.

Consulting companies can run up significant loans or creditors, and for poorly managed enterprises this can be an important factor that devalues the firm in the eyes of a buyer. Many sellers believe that with a few months' work, the footprint of loans and creditors can be minimized in the balance sheet. While this is true to some extent, the months of work can result in very little value in the sale process. This is because every accountant knows how to dress up a company for sale, and scrutiny of previous years' accounts will show readily how the company really works. This in turn will raise a question in the eyes of a buyer, and we will explore this later when we look at cash flow. The discipline of controlling liabilities should start at the very beginning of your enterprise, and not simply be applied for cosmetic reasons when you sell.

Liabilities can also sometimes be hidden from everyday view; for example, balloon payments on leases or contingent liabilities (which are liabilities that could occur if something else occurs, such as malpractice on breaking a confidentiality clause). An awareness of these liabilities is important, because they take constant management to avoid or minimize, and because they have the potential to take your negotiations with a buyer into a very subjective discussion, potentially protracting the sale process.

Finally, we come to the multiplier. The multiplier is the wildcard in your equation. It is a composite of several characteristics of your enterprise; its goodwill with clients, the stability of its workforce, the portfolio of clients, how long it is been operating successfully, and so on. It's a measure of reliability of the money-making machine.

At this point, most people have a quiet chuckle. We have been discussing an equation that appears to give you some certainty, as a seller, on how to value your enterprise. And there, right at the front of the equation, is a fuzzy number, a multiplier. Unfortunately that is the reality of the transaction. Any business—not just a consulting business—has intangible value, and this value should be factored into the calculation of a transaction price. For consulting, client relationships and goodwill are a large part of this intangible value.

Every accountant you speak to will have a different view of what the multiplier should be. Then again, every accountant you speak to has a different view on everything financial, so don't be surprised if you get multiple answers to your multiplier question. A good consulting enterprise will typically display strong goodwill, a stable workforce, a diverse portfolio of clients across economic sectors, a visible and strong footprint of repeat clients (clients who keep coming back to you), and a long history of successful and profitable operation. Such an enterprise might command a multiplier of between 2 and 3 (and sometimes more, in the right economic climate).

Now, if you know the left hand side of the equation (or how much you want to earn when you sell your enterprise), and if you promise yourself that you will never allow your liabilities to exceed your assets, then you can work out the average year's profit you need from your enterprise. Assume that your multiplier is 2, and you'll get a high estimate of average enterprise profit; assume that the multiplier is 3, and you'll get a low estimate of average enterprise profit. Your enterprise, then, will need to make an average annual profit of somewhere between the two numbers. It doesn't have to be exact, and you won't ever get it to be exact, but you will want to have quite a good sense of what this range is. It will be accurate enough for you to plan your enterprise toward an Exit Strategy.

This is really all you need. However, some sellers apply more sophisticated techniques to think more broadly about enterprise value. The broader perspective is useful. Some sellers calculate an internal rate of return, which financial professionals call the IRR. The IRR represents what the buyer might be able to do with the enterprise once he or she buys it, and how this translates into a return on capital invested. The IRR is a discounted cash flow calculation; in other words it considers, on the basis of an income profile over some time, how much should be paid in capital at the start to "buy" that income.

It is worth understanding the IRR of the transaction because it gives you an insight into the *relative* worth of your company compared with other options the buyer might have (such as starting their own firm, or acquiring a different firm, or investing in something else entirely). The calculation of an internal rate of return is well documented in many financial textbooks, so it will not be repeated here. For large enterprises that might operate for dozens of years, an IRR of 11%–14% might be considered reasonable. For smaller, shorter-lived investments, a higher IRR might be more suitable. Buyers have varying appetites for different IRRs, although industry norms do form around acceptable ranges, depending on the state of the economy. Accountants can provide insight into the industry and market norms at any given time.

If the buyer plans to do nothing with the enterprise and/or your annual profit is constant, then the IRR calculation might give you only slightly more insight than the enterprise value equation. But if the buyer might do something more than mine the profits of your enterprise—for example, leverage growth or facilitate an entry strategy into a new market for him or her—then it is worth considering the IRR. Also, if the buyer purchases your enterprise while it is still increasing its net profits (or, alternatively, decreasing) then the IRR calculation is quite useful to understand your potential negotiating stance. The IRR calculation is another useful data point which helps to clarify when in the life of your enterprise you can maximize your Exit Strategy outcomes.

A word of warning though. While the IRR is a useful vantage point, it will usually give you an inflated opinion of your enterprise value. The IRR signals what the long-term prospects for the firm are, and therefore the long-term value proposition for the transaction price at exit in the buyer's eyes. But in practical terms, the QEVE determines your true negotiating ground because it is firmly focused on short payback times and lowest-risk capital expenditure, while the IRR simply gives you insight into potential long-term upside value that you might argue over and above the QEVE outcome. I have met many entrepreneur consultants who have bemoaned this characteristic of the exit transaction of a consulting firm, telling me that it is "not fair" and that it violates standard capital IRR-based decision making. I have the same advice to them all. Get over it. Consulting is a service industry that is exposed to two prime risks; the potential and short-term ups and downs of a consulting practice, and the upturns and downturns of its clients. Why add a third risk—capital risk—if you can avoid it?

So, write down your QEVE answer in bold and your IRR answer in small font and in brackets.

When you work out your Exit Strategy, start with the numbers. Start with what number you want on the left hand side of the QEVE equation. This may be your retirement fund, or your nest egg to invest in other things, or simply a measure of the profit you want to make after some years of investment in your enterprise. Now, if this sounds like a not very inspirational way to start defining your Exit Strategy, don't despair. All you are doing at this stage is deciding what you want out of your entrepreneurial effort.

While the aforementioned description portrays a systematic and strategic approach, some successful consulting entrepreneurs did not think this way at the start. They simply rode their wave of success and exited when they were ready. Upon exit, they were either well placed to retire, or to start some new enterprises, or to change careers completely and follow a long-neglected passion. So they eventually got to do what they wanted after their exit. But every one of them, with the benefit of hindsight, agrees on this one point—if they had determined their exit value at the start, they might have been more successful, and they would almost certainly have arrived there more directly and in a shorter time.

CHALLENGE OF AN EXIT STRATEGY

Exiting a business is not as easy as exiting a café after you're done with your chocolate croissant and macchiato. There is a very important rule in Exit Strategies, and it is this: you have to be *allowed* to exit.

How does this work, if you're the boss? Surely you can walk away at any time? What's holding you back?

Let's work through it, because understanding this is crucial to how you exit, and therefore how you set your strategy from day one.

If a larger company—let's call them Heavy Hitters Inc.—buys out your enterprise, they are looking—at the very least—to continue your good work. More likely, they will be seeking to build on what you have achieved. Perhaps they want to integrate into another part of their company and create synergies that they never had. Perhaps they want to expand into new markets. The astute chief executive officer (CEO) of Heavy Hitters Inc. will want to leverage this deal so that it delivers more than what you've achieved.

Note, we have not said that this astute CEO will replace what you've achieved with something better. Unless you're selling a distressed asset at a bargain basement price (and we are not here to strategize toward *that* outcome!) they will want to keep the value that exists in your enterprise, and add to it, or leverage it up.

So they will look at where the money is coming from within your company. Now, if the revenue is largely attributed to you, your charismatic leadership, your exquisite deal-making skills, and your cutting-edge consulting acumen, there are two ways the deal could go.

One way is that they value your enterprise a whole lot less than it's really worth, because an important part of the machinery (you) is hell-bent on retiring to the Bahamas. Or you've been eating too many croissants and you're going to check out some other way. The point is, there is a bit of a risk that you're not going to be there tomorrow, and you're a bit too important for the buyer to ignore that. So there is a risk premium on the price of exit.

The other way is that, assuming that your health and longevity are not too much in question, the deal comes resplendent with your own personal bling, in the form of a "golden handcuff." The golden handcuff might include a clause that says they will pay you for the company over 3 years (or some other period that interferes with your flight bookings to the Bahamas), with the payment related to the profit that the company makes over those years. If your profit slides, so does the payment. And Mr., Ms., or Mrs. Heavy Hitter will make sure the penalty for sliding profits is high when your wrists are adorned with the "cuffs." Tight golden handcuffs won't pay you a simple third of the value every year; they will pay you, for example, 20% in year one, 35% in year two, and 45% in year three. In other words, most of your payout will occur toward the end of the term. It can be quite frustrating. There is a reason they are called golden handcuffs. You are, literally, a prisoner.

If you are happy with these outcomes—and some people are—then good for you. Carol, who exited her business successfully, subject to conditions that kept her in the business for 18 months after sale, says, "I thought of it as parole, not so much as incarceration. I was out, but I had to provide some direction and management in a nonexecutive board, with my final payment contingent on the company meeting some financial and personnel key performance indicators." Carol exited her enterprise elegantly despite the golden handcuff clauses. Yet there is scope to think more creatively. Most people do not want to be a prisoner of the buyer for 3 years after they have been the boss for the better part of a decade.

So how do we address this conundrum? We make you relatively unimportant in the organization at the point of sale. You are still the boss, but you're less of a president and more of a figurehead king or queen.

It's one thing to be *allowed* to exit, and it's another (much better) thing to be *encouraged* to exit. There is a lower likelihood of golden handcuffs being slapped on your wrists. So how do you set your strategy so that you will be encouraged to exit? Turning up to work without your pants will not do the trick; at least not in the way you expect it to. What is more likely to work is being a dead weight on the enterprise, a near-useless add-on who, unfortunately for Mr., Ms., or Mrs. Heavy Hitter, owns a lot of shares. While being a little bit dramatic to illustrate the point, it is nevertheless a useful and practical thing to aspire to.

As you will see throughout this book, you are indeed the life and soul of the enterprise, and the driving force behind the strategy. The key word is *behind*. If you, personally, are a largely invisible success factor in the current business, the buyer has to make some decisions. If others in your business are genuinely creating the successful outcomes in your business, and rightfully basking in the glory, the buyer has a conundrum to deal with. Do they keep you, with your considerable salary, associated costs and possibly redundant influence, or do they let you go?

The buyer will look at where the money is coming from, and if you're not in that part of the visible scenery, you're more likely to be encouraged to exit. This encouragement will occur quicker if the perception is that you're drawing a handsome salary and holding too many shares for your own good. It will be done with smiles and pomp and fanfare, it will be done more quickly, and you'll be on your way to the Bahamas with a warm feeling of goodwill, the buzz of good champagne and a healthier bank balance. An elegant exit.

Forming an Exit Strategy in which you're the first redundancy is a sublime way to move on and to maximize your returns. But it is not easy. On day one, you are the rainmaker, the daily grind machine, the accountant, the photocopier, the report binder, and the mailperson. On the day you exit, you want to be only slightly more useful than garden furniture in a

38th floor double-glazed office. How do you make that happen? Can you do it, or will your pride intervene? We'll come to that, but note for now that how you choose to make yourself less and less useful is an essential part of your Exit Strategy.

As you think about your Exit Strategy, allow yourself to visualize how your position in the company, and your control of the company, may change over time to allow you an elegant exit. To achieve what I have suggested earlier, the trajectory you take requires some relinquishment of the ego, as shown in Figure 2.3.

The elegance of your exit depends on a number of other factors. Earlier in this chapter, we touched on liabilities and debt. In addition to the obvious impact that debt has on valuation, getting out can be slow and laborious if your enterprise carries significant debt. After the global financial crisis in the late 2000s, tolerance for debt dissipated among the buyers of companies. Carrying debt brought deep suspicion and a paralyzing amount of due diligence from buyers. Financiers now wanted to check every minute detail of the debtor, down to DNA-level due diligence, before accepting debt-laden assets and enterprises. Debt went from being a load you could shoulder—in fact, once upon a time it made you look positively heroic and accountants applauded a well-geared balance sheet for its efficiency—to being the equivalent of deal-busting quicksand.

When you exit is as important as how you exit. Timing is key. Most enterprises are prone to two mistakes when it comes to timing. The first is

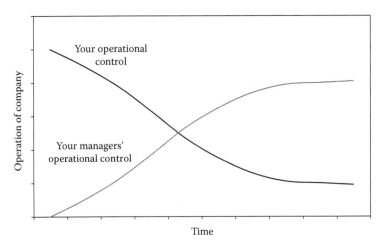

FIGURE 2.3
Healthy shift of operational control.

waiting too long. The second is exiting in a down market. Both mistakes drastically affect your negotiating platform at sale.

Entrepreneurs who wait too long often want to milk every ounce of success from their beloved enterprise. Your exit is quicker and provides more value for your time invested if you exit while your enterprise is still on its upward trajectory; when there is still more value to be gained without changing anything in your formula. Many entrepreneurs object to this. Surely, they argue, you can get more money if you ride the upward trajectory until it is at its peak? Surely then your enterprise is worth more?

The answer is yes, in theory. In practice, most buyers are astute enough to know that your company is at its peak, or that further value can only be gained if you change the formula. This leads to procrastination. Most sale processes take anywhere between 3 and 9 months to move from an expression of interest to settlement of the sale. In a consulting market, that is a reasonably long time. If your monthly revenues start plateauing or falling off, expect negotiations to be more iterative. The sale process is a reasonably disruptive one, both to your consulting enterprise and to you, the seller. The less iterative you make it, the less disruptive it is to your life. And iterations in negotiations are almost always instigated by the buyer.

Instead, you want to instill a sense of impatience in the buyer. You want your buyer to see your revenues increasing each month and each quarter; and you want your buyer to covet that increase. In tennis, timing your footwork and racket swing to hit the ball on the rise achieves your quickest and most efficient shot. Hitting the ball at its peak height, or as it is falling, requires more effort and loses time. The best sale timing, to entice buyers into committing quickly to maximize their short-term returns, is when your company is on a strong growth and revenue run, not at the end of the run when you have eked out maximum value for yourself. Clearly, the choice is yours—sell quickly on a strong run or risk selling with a more iterative negotiation process when the strong run is plateauing. But don't wait too long. Greed is *not* good for elegant exits (Figure 2.4).

The more obvious mistake—exiting in a down market—is easier to avoid. All markets fluctuate, and so will yours. It is sometimes attractive to consider selling when in a down market and times are hard. Your mindset can shift to an unhelpful place, one that muses *someone else can struggle through this dip; I've got a good consulting firm here and I will get a handsome return on investment, so let me cash out.*

Just like selling at the plateau of a revenue cycle, selling in a down market will be much more iterative than selling in a buoyant market. The sale

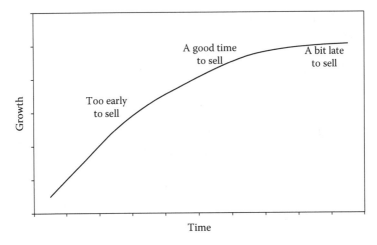

FIGURE 2.4
Timing your sale well.

process risks being less elegant and more disruptive as a result. Unless you have no option but to sell in a down market, avoid the prospect.

Instead, maintain resilience during a down market, and exercise patience so you time your exit on an upward trajectory.

Remember that buyers settle rapidly (even slightly impatiently); they pay well and there are more of them to fight over your enterprise when there is some way to go before you arrive at the peak of growth and profit performance. And if it is evident that you are on the right bearing to get there, and that you are in a buoyant market, you will be harassed to sell quickly.

While you have good control over when in your growth and profit performance you sell your enterprise, market forces can be fickle and you may not be blessed with the psychic ability to foresee the ups and downs. As you think about Exit Strategies, think about a simple business concept—limiting your company's sensitivity to market forces outside of your control.

So it is important to understand not just your business, but the business of your clients and the market forces that affect them. In other words, be an economist of sorts. In the absence of psychic powers, one way to reduce the risk of market forces upsetting your plans is to think about your client portfolio and apply basic economic logic to it. Create a safer environment for yourself by ensuring you have a balanced portfolio. If one client sector goes down, your business shouldn't dip at the same tangent or suffer unreasonably because of it. Minimize market risk.

Before I started my first enterprise I was working for one of the largest consulting firms on the planet. It had 110 offices globally. It had started in the 1970s with two entrepreneurs, and had grown over the decades to a firm with an A-list brand. I knew one of the founding entrepreneurs and had met the other on occasions. Stories about them were legendary to the point of being almost unbelievable. Once I actually met them, I found the stories quite plausible. They were impressive, visionary gentlemen. I had spent some time speaking with one of these men and had distilled, over two or three years, some gems of wisdom. These gems crystallized over time in my mind and, refined by my own thoughts and ideas, began to form a basic strategy.

One day, two colleagues, each with their own successful one-person consulting practice, took me out for dinner. They suggested I should do what they had done; hang out my shingle and join their band of one-man bands. We could form an alliance of sorts, they said. Provide each other with overflow work when one or the other was swamped. Synergy.

The red wine flowed freely and, having known each other for many years, the conversation was irreverent and funny. We formed a noisy table, overlooking a river on which ferry lights danced and the pinpoint-lighted silhouettes of bridges framed the evening sky.

Halfway through our third bottle of wine, deep into our second course, I declined their suggestion. I was in my mid-30s, with energy to burn, I said. Seven years on, I wanted to be able to retire if I chose. A one-person practice wasn't going to do that for me. A thirty or forty person practice might though. A hundred-person practice probably would.

I caught sardonic grins. What, in seven years?

Yep, I said. Set it up to sell from year one. And I think it can be done pretty easily, without much capital. I asked the waiter for his pen and some large sheets of paper, and explained my decision with an Exit Strategy. If you focus on the Exit Strategy, your mindset changes. Rather than simply focusing on a successful business, you focus on the build, and rate of build; and the stabilization and rate of stabilization. It makes you think differently, and I'd spent a couple of years thinking differently.

I scribbled some numbers, drew some graphs and somewhere in the process I sketched Spider-Man. In hindsight I'm not sure what Spider-Man had to do with my Exit Strategy. Perhaps I was suggesting that we could each be superheroes of our own destinies. (Did I mention the three bottles of wine?)

Less than eight years later, we had each done exactly that. We had each built enterprises of strength and value. It turns out it wasn't that hard to do once you had a vision in place, and the knowhow and determination to get there.

PREDICTING THE UNPREDICTABLE

A number of factors affecting your business are, to a lesser or greater extent, unpredictable. The longer you are in business, the greater the likelihood of some of these unpredictable factors visiting your enterprise. Your Exit Strategy must therefore be flexible in order to be resilient. Not so flexible that it disappears altogether when times change, of course. But the reality is that you may grow your enterprise faster or slower than you thought. Your succession planning may go well or poorly. The point here is that 7 or 10 or 15 years is a long time, and you should start by being supremely confident that at least some of your assumptions will turn out to be inaccurate.

Inaccuracy is not something to be feared. It is a fact of life, so anticipate it. In the world of process engineering in the 1980s, many analyses were created and evolved around the concept of process failures. They had names like fault tree analysis, and failure mode and event analysis. They were designed to systematically analyze where things could go wrong. Rather than ignoring the specter of failure, this discipline embraced it, became its friend and understood better how to avoid it. My favorite analysis tool was the unscientifically termed what-if analysis. Anyone could do this analysis, although its low entry threshold did mean that some fairly ridiculous what-if questions were asked. The operating rule for this analysis was "there are no stupid questions," mostly to alleviate the fear that might constrain people from asking questions that others might laugh at. But the strength of this analysis is that by encouraging participants to imagine failures and flawed assumptions, it created excellent insights into how to avoid blind spots. It even anticipated what professionals in the risk business call black swan events; those improbable but cataclysmic events that destroy companies.

Use the what-if analysis on your Exit Strategy. Question all the things you believe to be facts in your Exit Strategy, and then ask some more questions, no matter how improbable they seem. You will be amazed at how well you test your Exit Strategy. What if some enterprises had asked, "What if there is a global financial crisis?" or "What if climate change occurs?" or "What if there is a war in the Middle East?" Many companies that had no resilience to such possibilities, and consequently folded during dark economic periods, might have stood a better chance of surviving. Ask your family, friends, significant other, and any other trusted confidantes to help you wreck your Exit Strategy. You will be too close to the strategy to see some things, and you are likely to be defensive. They will ask questions that sit in your blind spot. They will also ask ridiculous questions, so be prepared for that. Good humor helps. You'll probably go back to the drawing board once or twice to finesse your Exit Strategy, because—unless you're a Grand Master of chess or a Zen strategist—your first attempt will have flaws that can be exposed. But it will benefit from this testing.

WHAT IS YOUR PRICE?

Your first estimate of sale value, using your QEVE equation, will not be your last estimate. It gets you into a ballpark but you now need to connect your cash out figure with your Exit Strategy. This is going to be iterative, because as you get into the exercise and you build your plan, you'll change it.

Let's start with the cash out figure. You may find that you become very confident that you can achieve the first number, and you might revise it upward. Or you might find that it takes too long to achieve the first number, and you revise it downward. Everyone's number will be different. Be reasonably specific. If you simply want to be a millionaire, that's too vague. How many millions of dollars? 1.5 million? 4.0 million? 7.3 million? 17 million? It is useful to think about what you want to do with the money, and then work backward. What do you want to do when you exit? Put the kids through university? Pay off your mortgages and buy other properties? Invest in start-up companies? Spend a lot of time on a beach? Live off the interest of the remainder? Start a new career path? Become a perennially unpaid artist or writer? Some of the above? All of the above?

It's part daydreaming and part analysis, but it gives you the first data point in your vision. You should have a number. Without it, you don't have an anchor for your analysis.

From this number, you'll work out the average profit your enterprise has to make 3 years running (at least) for you to be reasonably confident that you can hit that number. You'll have a lower and upper bound by now, because the goodwill multiplier might be at the lower or upper end of the scale. You might overlay this with your IRR analysis, if you have a very good idea of what an astute buyer might want to do with the enterprise you create.

Now you want to figure out how you become redundant in this enterprise over that period of time, unless of course you accept that a golden handcuff is part of your Exit Strategy.

Becoming redundant is a very tricky proposition, particularly if you also want to be able to positively and compellingly influence the realization of your Exit Strategy at the time of your exit. You need to have enough management control, and enough shareholder voting rights, to steer the outcome in the direction you need. But at the same time, in order to become redundant, you have to give away some (and probably a sizeable portion) of management control to others in your staff. So this means that by the time you are ready to execute your Exit Strategy, you'll want to have people who do what you do (and perhaps they do what you do even better than you do it yourself).

Although it is theoretically possible to hold 100% of the shares at the time of your Exit Strategy, this is not a practical expectation to have unless you are resigned to a golden handcuff or are particularly lucky. Your people should have skin in the game—a reason to stay and make the Exit Strategy work—during the potentially tumultuous period of sale and your exit. If your key people don't have equity in the outcome of the sale, there is a greater likelihood that your enterprise will crumble. Key people might leave, and in that scenario you cease to become redundant. We will discuss, in Chapter 9, some ways of minimizing this risk, but the most effective tactics need plenty of time to implement—and shareholding is one such decision that you should make early. So an important part of your thinking has to be the shape of the equity holdings at your time of exit, which is related to your potential structure at the time of exit. And this, in turn, is related to your consulting model, the number of offices you have, and the practices you run within your enterprise. Of course, you're not a psychic so you don't know these with any kind of confidence when you start your enterprise. So you make assumptions. Now, hopefully, you can see why the calculations are iterative. There are a few parameters to think through, and you can virtually guarantee that all of them will vary from your base assumptions.

If you have less than 100% of the shares, then it stands to reason that the real dollar amount you, personally, get from selling is less than the figure you started estimating with. This is one of the reasons your planning will be highly iterative. You will want to revisit the QEVE equation several times. Be prepared to map scenario after scenario, and commit to patient and careful consideration of your analysis. Go back to the exit number and alter it—over and over—until you get what you want, with the distributed shareholdings.

Quite some time later, you've run quite a few spreadsheets. You've got variables on multipliers and variables on shareholding arrangements. You've got at least one, and perhaps several, thumbnail sketches of the corporate structure at exit. You've got what-if scenarios. After a while, with all of this elasticity tested and varied, you've got a sense of how robust your plan is.

Scientists have a way of making sense out of lots of what-if scenarios. They have a method of analysis called the Monte Carlo analysis, which runs variable after variable, and change after change of assumptions, until a set of likely outcomes becomes evident. Monte Carlo analyses run millions of such scenarios. Obviously, you won't have time to run millions of analyses, but you should try to assess as many scenarios as you can, until you become confident that you can see a set of likely outcomes, and you are comfortable with the spread of these potential outcomes.

CREATING FLEXIBILITY

You might quite sensibly ask at this point if it's possible to do all this without knowing *exactly* what type of consulting you (the enterprise) are going to be doing at the point of exit. Yes it is, because these analyses will cause you to think about the core consulting competencies you'll need to create to get to this Exit Strategy. Of course, you'll need to know *generally* what type of consulting organization you are considering (what discipline) and what service model you are thinking of (value based, knowledge based, body-shopping or a hybrid), but at this point you don't need precise detail. We're still creating an Exit Strategy, not a business plan.

The debilitating trap here is to think at this point that you cannot achieve the Exit Strategy number you would like to, and you revise your thinking downward. If you had a healthy Exit Strategy number, you will have what looks like a daunting enterprise to create. But if you think small you'll achieve small, so keep thinking as big as you need. Think like an entrepreneur. Spend more time and determination working out how you can achieve your preferred Exit Strategy outcome, rather than altering your Exit Strategy to suit your conservatism.

Endurance athletes focus on one step at a time. If they contemplated the hill above them during the race, they would feel slightly dismayed. In that dismayed mindset, in order to overcome the hill, they would need to increase their mental strength and wattage considerably. They will run a much more effective race if they are not burdened with a dismayed feeling during the event; if they concentrate on their one-step-at-a-time focus.

Before the race, however, endurance athletes contemplate the hills and they visualize how to get over them. They contemplate the enormity of the challenge. They don't ruefully accept a pessimistic outlook and seek smaller hills or a different race to participate in. But during the race, they focus on the plan, one step at a time.

It's worth mentioning the possibility that your Exit Strategy can also take the form of selling out to your staff—a management buyout. It is possible, but it is a slightly longer shot to meet your cash out value than selling out to Heavy Hitters Inc. If you build a capital asset worth a significant amount of money, then it is possible that for many salaried people—your people—the price of a decent shareholding in such a company might be similar to a mortgage. And given that many of your staff might already be shouldering the burden of a mortgage, you may not find many buyers in your company that add up to the capital amount you seek.

To overcome this, you could sell slowly. Selling down a little bit every year can make the proposition more attractive to your staff, but this is not much different to a golden handcuff. In addition, this introduces internal politics to your Exit Strategy, which is counterproductive. Perhaps several staff members hope to be managing director when you leave. Incremental equity sales to staff with the intention of allowing you to exit, creates plenty of room for maneuvering in the ranks of your employees. The time taken to think of these maneuvers detracts from the time taken to make the business a profitable entity. Your first priority should be to maintain a high and consistent profitability, and a strong growth trajectory. This requires client focus by your staff, not a focus on internal shareholding and jostling for position. Overall, and despite its validity as an option, this option comes with several significant challenges that affect the execution of your Exit Strategy. And if you consider the market, a management buyout limits your market to one buyer; an internal consortium. It does not lend itself to competitive forces that, in turn, can help push up your sale value.

If you are looking to sell your company to a bigger firm, then part of forming your Exit Strategy (before you start your company) is to look at who's buying what in your market and why. There has—in my experience over the last 25 years, including on either side of the global financial crisis—been considerable acquisition activity in the consulting market. So there is a lot of information to be gathered, and much of it has a local or national flavor, as well as differences depending on whether the consulting is in the legal, engineering, financial, or other sectors. The intelligence gathering takes time, so be prepared to invest in research. It is likely that you will find different scales of transactions. For example, you might find that the number of consultancies of around 20 staff that are acquired is very high, and that there were fewer acquisitions of companies with staff of 100 or more. You might find that mergers, rather than acquisitions, occur in the larger companies. This type of intelligence helps you to understand what buyer targets you might need to consider in executing your Exit Strategy.

It is worth doing a case study on an acquisition. This is best done from a seller's perspective. Spending time with principals who have sold their companies is a very enlightening experience. Understanding what they would have done similarly or differently if they could wind back the clock is a very useful exercise for you to undertake. Throughout this book, you will see glimpses of the reflections of successful entrepreneurs who have been down that path.

If you speak to enough of them, you'll absorb a diversity of opinion, and you'll see common themes. One of the very important observations is about preserving the company culture. If you have spent time and energy building a successful consulting firm, the last thing you need is for the sale process to fray its successful culture. Selling a company can be debilitating for staff, particularly if you have built the company from scratch. Like it or not, you become the patriarch or the matriarch, and leaving your herd can be disconcerting for your staff. It can be disconcerting for you too.

Some of your staff might feel abandoned, and many will feel fear and uncertainty. These are natural feelings, and anticipating them when you start your enterprise is valuable.

There will be a compulsion for some people to leave, or at the very least to look around for other opportunities, when you announce your intention to sell. Do not for one minute assume you can spring this as a surprise on your staff. They will know when you begin negotiating to sell, probably within days or weeks of your first serious courting of buyers. When you embark on the process of selling (which can take many months), trust becomes your ally in retaining staff, so prepare for openness. But even with transparency and your best attempts at gaining trust, expect some loss of staff. In Chapter 9, we look at how to manage both the loss, and the disruption of loss.

It's important then, with this expected attrition, to avoid key person risks. Key person risks occur when the value of your company becomes concentrated around one or two or a small handful of individuals. Once again, thinking about these issues at the start of your enterprise might help you to structure your company to minimize this risk.

Nick ran one of the more nimble consulting enterprises you will find— advertising. For sheer speed, creativity and volatility, there is no match. It must be the quintessential bucking bronco of consulting. Long before *Mad Men* was a television success in the late 2000s and early 2010s, Nick had his own successful firm. His enterprise model pivoted around very creative people who occupied General Manager roles. It seemed to succeed exceedingly well, but in an unstructured way. The three Creative Directors in his firm were celebrated heroes as they won wave after wave of advertising campaigns from big name firms; the other fifty or so staff were not. The Creative Directors would find ideas that were often breathtaking, and The Others would painstakingly turn those ideas into wonderful campaigns.

Nick's enterprise had developed a class system. There were four heroes, including Nick, and then there were The Others. The four heroes landed lucrative contracts. They were prominent in the organization, and The Others worked in the background. Nick later admitted that the pay gap and the equity gap between the heroes and The Others were quite wide.

When Nick began processes to sell his firm, The Others began to leave. One by one, then small group by small group. Nick made an attempt to introduce a new equity model, and succeeded in stemming the flow of his valuable employees, the ones who turned ideas into TV and magazine campaigns. But he had lost a noticeable percentage, and the sale negotiation process seemed more protracted. He sold his firm, successfully, in the end, at a lower price than he had hoped for.

Two years after the sale, I interviewed Nick. He was philosophical. "We were so successful, but I neglected the majority of staff. I had two classes of employees. The ones I relied upon for hard work, rather than creativity, were disillusioned. When they started leaving, [the buyer] revised the price. This happened three times in total, and the contract negotiations went on for 18 months. It was a tough lesson, and a mistake I will not make again."

CELL MODEL

Let us look at structuring your company to achieve flexibility and resilience, and how this might work. We will explore this in detail in Chapter 4, but for now let's get the philosophy embedded in your thinking, at the very start of your enterprise planning.

There are two mantras that are worth living by. One is, resource for the troughs in demand, not the peaks. The other is, spread your risk by creating diverse services. Both of these mantras can be lived, in your consulting enterprise, by thinking in cells.

One of the useful lessons of guerrilla warfare, dating back to the Boer War in South Africa, and in the widespread terrorism of the twenty-first century, is the concept of cells. The operation of a cell structure allows mobility and connectedness, without the rigidity that comes with a classical pyramid structure. Importantly, if you remove one cell, the organization still functions, because it can continue to perform its activity unimpeded, and with relatively little loss of institutional capability.

In entrepreneurial consultancy, thinking about your consulting offerings in cells gives you flexibility and resilience. It is not likely to give you market power, because your capacity within each cell might be relatively small. However, if each cell undertakes a consulting activity that relates to other cells, but can also undertake assignments independently of other cells, you can create a potent collection of cells, and therefore a potent enterprise. The more cells you have with similar strengths and abilities, the more resilient your enterprise is to the loss of one or two cells, or a downturn that affects one or two cells.

In the previous section, we discussed the risk of people leaving, and the key person risks you might carry. You can "anchor" your cells better, and further reduce attrition risk, by providing equity or other incentives to the leaders of your key cells well before selling. For holders of equity, in particular, the financial incentive to stay can be quite powerful. This is because the acquiring firm sees an upside to buying your company; growth or consolidation or some other value-accruing mechanism. That may mean that Heavy Hitters Inc. believes that its investment might be doubled or tripled in a few years (say 5 years). Any shareholders who are in the company prior to sale should benefit from the post-sale aspirations of Heavy Hitters Inc.—a good incentive to stay.

If you create a cell model, you will become focused on the flexibility and resilience of your company cell by cell, which breaks down the larger problem into smaller, bite-sized problems.

SYSTEMS AND PROCESSES

At the start of an entrepreneurial activity, there seems little need for systems and processes. In fact, your enterprise can operate quite well, and efficiently, without too many of these.

Although there is genuine warmth about running your enterprise like a family business, the reality is that a larger company acquiring your company will probably have more impersonal systems and processes. They might have a more overt hierarchy, possibly even stronger governance, and possibly some centralized control. Anticipating these, and gently building your company so that your staff are not left with a sour feeling of dreaded anticipation at systems, governance, and hierarchy helps to prevent culture shock. Ben, an organizational psychologist, attributes much of the turnover in personnel that is observed in sale processes to the impending change in culture. "Small, or medium-sized enterprises attract and retain people who become used to working in flexible environments. It becomes a comfort zone for them. When a larger company buys a smaller company, the employees of the smaller firm often feel a sense of dread that they are going into a 'machine.' In reality, few people actively dislike structure and form, but the change from a flexible environment to a more regimented environment often has people looking for alternatives." Ben's suggestion is to "wean them" onto systems, processes, and the other trappings of a larger firm.

An effective and productive way to do this is to have your cell leaders create systems and governance. Emulate the systems and governance processes of your key clients. Your staff will learn to work with client processes, and will learn to pick the best from the smorgasbord of processes that they are exposed to. And in building processes, they will own them and be much more wedded to them. Your enterprise wins in two ways here. First, by emulating key client processes (particularly the larger companies' processes) it is likely that your staff will be much less daunted when Heavy Hitters Inc. flaunts its processes. If your staff has worked with BP's or GSK's or Nestle's processes, they will not be daunted by a large or midtier consulting firm's processes. Second, you'll build strong professionalism in your enterprise, and you might even find a slight upward bump in your multiplier as a result.

There is, of course, more to Exit Strategies than this, and the remaining chapters deal with them. But the main reflection is this: with nothing in place, with no functioning business and just the wisp of an idea in your head, don't feel sheepish about thinking in detail about your Exit Strategy. It will change how you think about your enterprise, and your wisp of a good idea will grow into a behemoth of a great vision. It won't do that overnight, like some Jack-and-the-Beanstalk sorcery, but it will grow. And the more time you spend on it, the more it will grow. Be patient and don't start your story until you know the ending intimately.

THREE TIPS

Tip 1: Work out the capital value of your exit, and be prepared to recalculate it several times—before you start your enterprise, and after. Be clear about what you want your life to look like after you've achieved the sale and exit, because this vision—and not the dollar amount—is what will continue to inspire you.

Tip 2: Be clear about how you will extract yourself from your firm at the point of exit. It is easy to be vague about this topic. Don't. Take your exit position very seriously, try to make yourself redundant by developing your staff to be the true drivers of your enterprise—or be prepared for a golden handcuff clause in your sale contract.

Tip 3: Think through how you maximize the enterprise value at exit through the retention of key staff. When you leave, you want your staff to see this as an opportunity to advance their careers and financial position; not as a sign that your enterprise is ending its run.

3

Finding and Keeping Consultants

The best way to find yourself is to lose yourself in the service of others.

Mahatma Gandhi

TYPECASTING CONSULTANTS

Consulting is a service industry. Don't let anyone ever tell you differently. And if you think it is anything else, don't try to create a consulting enterprise. You would have started the journey of growing and selling a successful consulting firm with your shoelaces tied together.

Consulting is a service industry and, because of this, its brand value is significantly influenced by goodwill. The goodwill comes from customer satisfaction. The customer satisfaction comes not just from the outcome of a consulting assignment, but also from the customer's experience in reaching the outcome.

Many consulting enterprises fail because they eventually forget this fundamental truth. They get caught up in billings, billability, chargeable hours, and winning projects, and they forget that the foundation stone of their enterprise is great service. It's doing the task that they are assigned to do, in a way that clients feel reassured about. That is not to say, of course, that billings and winning projects aren't crucial. Your consulting enterprise has to be commercial. But every time you do great work with great customer service, you cement your enterprise into a solid brick. Keep doing this and your enterprise will not be made out of straw; and it will not easily succumb to the external huffing and puffing of a fickle marketplace.

Good service requires humility. Herein lies the conundrum. You see, consultants solve problems (well, good consultants do, anyway). To solve some of the problems that consultants face, the person will need to have some special skills. After all, if just *anyone* could solve the problem at hand, no one would call this consultant. So a good consultant knows that he or she is quite talented. If consultants are talented, and if they get paid well for solving problems that other mortals struggle with, you can see why it's difficult for them to be humble. The loss of humility is collateral damage. This is why the consulting world seems to be populated by arrogant and condescending individuals. Being a top-gun, humble consultant is a contradiction in terms.

But the conundrum gets worse. These consultants do all this in a competitive environment where other smart people compete with them. They are going to wilt unless they have egos the size of Africa. Why? Because these consultants have to convince their prospective clients that their special skills are simply more impressive than the other consultant's special skills. Remember, when pitching for work, most consultants don't always know what the answer to the client's problem is. But a good consultant needs to have enough mojo to impress their client that they will probably find an answer, better and faster than the other consultant. Good consultants need confidence in that ability. All of this adds up to quite an attitude tightrope.

Now, you—their leader—want to create an enterprise with 20, 100, or 200 of these egotistical beings. You want them to positively rock in the marketplace, to be confident in pitching and selling, to attract others like them to your enterprise. And you want them to focus, first and foremost, on exemplary service. You are trying to recruit thoroughbred racehorses, and you're asking them to humbly serve clients like dependable Clydesdales.

This is your cultural dilemma.

When looking for consultants, you are looking for a balance of ability, confidence, and a service mentality—and these people are rare.

Why aren't there many of them around? Because most consulting firms forget that they are service industries. If you can remember that fact, and build a service mentality deep into your company's DNA, you will build a strategic advantage in the market. It won't seem like it because it accrues slowly. It's not the hero model. There is no fanfare. It is the tortoise to the hare. But eventually, your service mentality will show, and it will show as strategic advantage. In addition, this strategic advantage is not something that others can turn on like a lightbulb. Once you have it, and others don't, it will take a long time before those competitors build their own service mentality and compete effectively against your strategic advantage. You may even find that buyers who are missing that strategic advantage will want to buy your enterprise partly because of that mojo you have created.

But you have to build that service industry ethic without losing the ego. A consultant's ego is a weapon of choice, and something to be nurtured. Muhammad Ali's ego set him up for greatness. He didn't believe he would just be average. He figured he would be the best. There wasn't a lot of humility in his demeanor. Usain Bolt didn't contemplate being the second fastest man alive; his ego told him he would be the fastest man alive. Ego is a powerful attribute because it allows the aspirational to be imagined and the improbable to be accomplished. Consultants with healthy egos are good for business.

Of course, a healthy ego without the intellect that is essential to consulting is a liability, not an asset. You want your consultants to be smart, in order to justify the ego. Smart people can be found everywhere. There are many smart people in government, many smart people in industry and many smart people in academia. In each of these sectors, it is possible to survive and thrive even if you are not particularly smart. However, in consulting, it is difficult to thrive without being smart.

So we have established a trademark of a typical good consultant. An admirable IQ, quick with that mind. Confident in solving problems. Competitive and probably egotistical. Hopefully with a service mentality to go with all of that.

Ben, the organizational psychologist we met earlier, puts it this way: "We talk about IQ and EQ. In a service industry like consulting, IQ gives you the client outcomes that they pay for. EQ gives you the client experience that they come back for. If you want repeat work, build the EQ of your people."

There is an often-quoted statistic that goes like this: it takes four times as much expense and effort to find a new client as it does to keep existing clients. Whether it's two times, four times, or ten times, the message is the same: It's just bad business to have client turnover that you can attribute to average or poor service. Some people call this "client churn." While "client churn" sounds painful for the clients, it is actually far more painful for the consultants. In reaching your Exit Strategy, you want to accrue good clients, not cycle through them. Even if some clients do not have much work for you one year, nurture them. Keep them in your client bank like a term deposit, somewhere in the background, looked after and not forgotten. You want every client you've ever had to think of you first when they have work to outsource.

So you need to ask yourself two questions. Are you consultant material? And, in building your consulting enterprise, can you find enough consulting-material types? Only you can answer the first, and the answer to the second is absolutely yes, provided you can answer the first with a yes.

Why have we made such a big deal about the service mentality, that balance between ego and humility, and you? Your consulting staff will follow your lead. They will watch you and emulate you. So this balance needs to start with you. If your staff haven't got the service mentality down pat, you will spend huge amounts of your precious time smoothing over gradually worsening client relationships. You will expend effort fighting the gentle erosion of your goodwill multiplier in our quick enterprise value estimate (QEVE) equation. You will struggle to march relentlessly toward your Exit Strategy because the ground below you gets steadily more slippery from the ooze of client frustration. If you want to build a consulting empire and not age like you're maturing in dog years, ensure that your staff gets the client service right. Otherwise, the road is difficult. It's no fun, after you've exited, to be a thirty- or forty-something millionaire and look like you're seventy, with bad ulcers and a worse heart.

Your route to your exit is much smoother and easier if your staff provide exemplary client service in addition to knowledge, analysis, and insight.

So the selection of your consultants, the role modeling you provide them personally, and the role modeling you ensure your key leaders provide are the essence of your success. This defines the culture of your company, and everything else, as we'll see, is merely tactical support in getting you to your Exit Strategy.

When Josh was selling his consulting practice, a new managing director was running the firm in the few weeks between the contract agreement and the settlement date. Josh was on a family holiday in Australia during that time. He had a long distance call on his cell phone that woke him up at 3 am. It was a valued client Josh had known for almost 6 years, calling from many time zones away. For the next 20 minutes the client recounted the way his project was "unraveling." Josh knew that it had hit a couple of hurdles, which was not unexpected. These sorts of hurdles had been encountered before, but never with this much drama from the client. The client was frustrated and angry. Josh suggested he approach the new managing director to walk him step by step through the hurdles and what was being done, explaining to the client that during the sale process he no authority to intervene. Josh gave him a sympathetic ear, but could not offer much else. "Privately, I thought the problems and the solutions being applied matched well, and my previous staff were applying the same intellectual rigor as ever before. But something had changed in the way they communicated with and empathized with this client," he recalled. Josh relayed the information to the new managing director after the client had hung up, and recalls an offhand reception to the news. Josh reflected later how easy it was to change a company's service mentality for the worse, in just a few short months. Less than 6 months later, after a long and faithful association with Josh's consulting firm, this client took his business to another consulting firm.

TAXONOMY OF MUST-HAVE CONSULTANTS

It is surprising how many people—even seasoned consultants—think that all consultants are cut from roughly the same cloth. Nothing could be further from the truth. If you are going to build a successful consulting firm, you will achieve it more quickly and efficiently if you recognize and strategically build your firm using the different types of consultants that are available to you.

Quite aside from client service, there are four attributes that are vital to building a high-performance consulting team. Two are client related and two are assignment related.

The two client-related attributes are securing the client and keeping the client. These attributes are demonstrated by what we'll term hunters and farmers, respectively. The two assignment-related attributes are innovation and completion. They appear in what we'll call *creatives* and *closers*. The four categories of consultants are therefore hunters, farmers, creatives, and closers. We will look at them in more detail in this chapter. These categories are not mutually exclusive, just as introversion and extroversion are not mutually exclusive. It is quite normal for good consultants to display two or more of these characteristics, and for them to have clear preferences.

How much of each of the four attributes you will need in your consulting firm will depend on your clients, sectors, the type of consulting you do (body shopping, knowledge based, value based, or hybrid), and the types of assignments or contracts you typically engage in. The mix will vary too, as your firm grows and matures. Let us look at each type in turn.

The hunter is, as the name suggests, the traditionally recognized rainmaker who attracts clients or wins contracts. The hunter is the glamourpuss of consulting and is often harnessed by sales or business development functions in larger firms. He or she wins clients through great business development and through finding the value proposition that the client has not had before. The hunters have a competitive edge that keeps them hungry. They are the high-fivers of your empire, and their ego is extremely well developed. They find gratification in the hunt and the win (or the "kill," as some of them will actually call it). They see themselves at the top of the food chain, and you will often hear them pointing out (usually during salary and bonus reviews) that if not for them, the company would have no clients.

The hunters see themselves as the Alphas. This is not a bad thing, if you consider what their primary job in your firm truly is. The core of their job is to be effective in competitive scenarios and to win contracts. They sell well. They direct the clients' attention to the best parts of the consulting approach, the winning strategy. They accentuate the competitive advantages of your company's problem-solving strategy and instill confidence in the client. They are celebrated heroes and—like all four of your categories—deserve to be so. But if you are not careful, the hunters can inadvertently apply a default setting to your culture simply because they are so visible and persuasive. And, while there is nothing wrong with that culture, you may not necessarily want that as your default setting. Recall Nick, the advertising executive, who had five celebrated hunters, and his suboptimal sale process.

The farmer is a lot less conspicuous in your organization. He or she guides the clients through their problems and their solutions. The farmer is there every day, with both the mundane and the exciting parts of the assignments, a constant in the ebb and flow of the relationship that might see difficult days. The farmer is the after sales service, the essence of the clients' experiences with your firm. Farmers delight in elegant solutions and in a job well done. They see beauty in well-oiled machinery. They worry if the assignment is less profitable than it should be. Farmers are the stewards of your consulting empire, and many often do not see it, overshadowed as they are by their A-lister hunter compatriots.

The farmers often see themselves as the quiet achievers. Farmers gather repeat work and harvest the loyal customers by giving them a reason to be loyal. Clients warm to the farmers because they become familiar and trustworthy. They put the clients' interests ahead of less noble things than billable hours and profitability, and clients sense this. The farmer sees cross-selling opportunities (the opportunities to sell different services into the same client firm) readily, because they begin to read the needs and the nuances of the client firm. Farmers give you, the chief executive officer (CEO) of your enterprise, the most valuable intelligence and insights into your clients' current and future problems, and allow you to position well to extend your services there. If hunters give you the ability to grow in infrequent but spectacular sprints, farmers give you the ability to effect compound growth steadily every day.

In the beginning, as you begin to build your consulting firm, it is natural to have a stronger reliance on hunters. As you break into the market, connecting with new clients and attempting to convert those connections into contracts, hunters are essential. As your firm grows, maintain an analytical eye on the amount of work that comes in from hunters, and the amount of work that comes in from farmers. If your client stewardship is strong and your performance on assignments is excellent, you should notice a great deal of work coming in from repeat assignments or cross-marketing within client organizations. In many cases, the revenues attributable to farmers can outstrip the revenues attributed to hunters. Irrespective of the balance you find in your organization, ensure that you understand what it is, and what potential you have between your hunters and your farmers to increase revenues from your marketplace.

Let us now look at the other two types of consultants—the ones that actually deliver a large measure of the professional outcomes.

Creatives are your smart problem solvers. They live for the unique solutions to the rare and difficult problems. They work best in complexity. Sometimes they will look for a complicated solution when a simple one stares them in the face. They are usually at the cutting edge of knowledge, a position they keep through the sheer force of their own thirst for creative power. Creatives come in all shapes and sizes, from the antisocial tech-nerd to the extroverted ball of energy with the slight behavioral problem. Their Achilles' heel is their tendency to boredom. Once they see the solution, they develop ADD. They need another space in which to develop another new and innovative solution to a problem that mere mortals struggle mightily with. The concept is all, and the last line drawn on the road map marks the end of their journey. They don't need to live the solution. They just need to see it and capture its essence.

You don't need many of these high maintenance creatives, but you do need some. Your consulting brilliance is parked right here. But you need to manage very carefully how many of them you have in your firm. People with ideas are innovative gold, but their ADD-like tendencies are a serious productivity issue. Someone else will need to actually provide the long tail of consulting service that winds behind the genius concept.

Closers get the job done. They will slog. If success is 20% inspiration and 80% perspiration, meet the sweaty guys. They have focus, and an almost unbreakable 1000-yard stare for the finish line. They have tenacity and an uncanny ability to stretch time, creating great final products under intense schedule pressures. They are the engine of your well-oiled machinery, marathon runners rather than sprinters, both efficient and effective. Every closer you have can probably go out into the market on their own and make a successful solo career or small business in consulting. Simply because they get the job done. They have no Achilles' heel.

The attention to detail that closers bring to your organization will make the difference between a good job and a great job. A great job is where the finish is perfect, the ending is as it should be. The closer is the difference between the client who says "they did a good job and we just had a little bit of tidying up at the end to get their solution into play" and the client who says "next time, I'd be happy to go on vacation while these guys are completing the assignment. It met specification perfectly."

If you map your types out on a two-by-two grid, you will find consultants group something like Figure 3.1.

Let us look at the combinations of types.

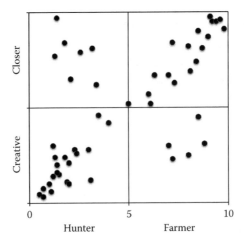

FIGURE 3.1
Types of consultants.

Creative-hunters are your business development agents who often flourish in the private-sector client world, finding competitive edges and winning work prolifically. They find new business and new clients, and are often best when they are forging new frontiers. Closer-farmers are your client stewards, delivering the work no matter where the work is won, whether it is from the private sector or the public sector. They get repeat business from their clients because of the exemplary delivery and client stewardship.

Creative-farmers are good at finding cross-marketing opportunities within existing client organizations. They can leverage good service to widen the scope of activity within a given client organization. Closer-hunters are particularly good at finding competitive edges in public tenders, where tenacity and strategic thinking are needed in roughly equal measure. It is not the most inspiring of hunting assignments, but it is complex and demanding ... and often yields high revenue assignments that contribute to a surge in growth.

When you start your consulting empire, you need to play all four roles of hunter, farmer, creative, and closer. It is a busy period of your life, because all four hats are difficult to wear simultaneously. As your empire grows, you find "specialists" that fall into these categories. Your ability to recognize them for what they are, and what they can be, will be one of your leadership attributes that will help to create a successful consulting practice.

A common error that consulting leaders make is that they do not have a clear model with which to define excellence along these two axes in Figure 3.1. Consequently, they make two mistakes in running their firm. The first is that they expect people to shine in all roles ("go find work in new markets, and cross market with existing clients, be innovative and make sure you lock down every last detail"). You see how ridiculous that sounds, and yet that expectation is endemic in the consulting world. Those that can fulfill three of the four are earmarked for leadership, which is a good thing—but it leaves a lot of talent undeveloped. There are excellent consultants around who are not a Jack of all trades; they have a niche and they perform very well in that niche. Recognizing the less obvious but arguably no less valuable talent and growing a consulting firm with depth is key to being a successful consulting leader.

The second mistake the consulting leaders make is that they predominantly reward creative-hunters, and are less generous toward closer-hunters, creative-farmers, and closer-farmers. This incentivizes only a fraction of the company to perform, and it can lead to insidious cultural problems. The most obvious of these is the problem encountered by Nick, the advertising consultant in Chapter 2—a class system and a subsequent disenchantment (and eventual exodus) of the less celebrated classes. Less obvious, but equally impactful, is the slow deterioration of the service mentality of the firm. You are rewarding sales but not service delivery and client stewardship skills. Eventually—over a period of 3 or 4 years if you evaluate remuneration and pay bonuses annually—you build a car dealership mentality rather than a service mentality.

We have spent some time identifying the attributes of good consultants, and how they fit in a successful consulting firm. All leaders are also acutely aware of the virtues of hiring good people, and hiring well. However, there is an aspect of consulting that lends itself to hiring poorly. This is the concept of the billable consultant. The billable consultant dutifully chews through work for the client in a (hopefully) satisfactory manner and creates revenue. Provided the revenue keeps coming—in other words the consultant is "billable," many consulting firms are quite relaxed about how good that consultant actually is. These invisible consultants, often found in larger firms, are like "filler" material.

"Filler" consultants are reasonably disposable and easily replaceable. The economics of consulting—in which the charge-out rate is many multiples of the salary cost—means that if the "filler" consultants are being billed to clients, they add continually to the bottom line. Provided they are doing this, many consulting leaders do not consider whether or not they add to the capability of the firm. Little is done to choose them well, little is done to develop them, and if the workload falls, they can be let go. This is a consistent, and often disengaging, aspect of the consulting industry. The first sign that a consulting firm is hiring "filler" material is when you hear something like, "I don't care, I just need a business consultant who can analyze debt and equity, get me one quickly." It shows that the hirer is looking to fill a short-term gap rather than choose talent for the long term. He or she might be better off engaging a higher-cost, temporary contractor and reserving the permanent hiring activity for when there is time to choose carefully.

Danielle, a consultant who left her firm to practice as a lone consultant, reflects on her time in "Big Consulting." "I felt like a workhorse," she recalls. "If we weren't billing 40 or more hours a week, we were reviewed. Questions were asked of us, and of our managers. To cover our salaries and overheads, we had to bill 18 hours a week minimum. So if we billed between 18 and 30 hours a week, we were kind of tolerated.

We were profitable, but we also knew that we were not really valued." Her story will sound familiar to many consultants. Consulting firms can develop a factory culture that can be deeply disengaging for many staff, who eventually feel like "filler" material. And while it is—from a short-term financial perspective—clearly a profitable way to operate, is it a wise model to use if you are attempting to build a successful consulting practice?

To build a high-value small-to-medium–sized firm—or even a large firm—the kind of model that fills gaps with just any billable consultants should be viewed as intrinsically inefficient over the long term. Unlike government or private industry, where there are many roles and functions that support the strategic purpose of the organization, consulting is a tighter labor force. Because it is a service industry, its success depends on undertaking relatively short, outcome-oriented tasks, many of which are underpinned by a vexing problem. Consulting units are like strike teams, with relatively little space for noncore functions. Consulting—at the small-to-medium entrepreneur scale—does not have a great deal of labor redundancy, nor a great deal of support infrastructure compared with larger private industry or government. And so the most productive consulting model is when you have the lowest number of personnel required to deliver the required client outputs. It is also the most resilient consulting firm to build, and forms the strongest foundations for continuous growth.

As a consulting CEO, it is important to understand the labor force and notice the key hunters, farmers, creatives, and closers. It is important to be effective and efficient, and to look within your employees for the talents that can be nurtured. If you are building a firm and you find yourself wondering if you have "filler" material despite your best efforts to hire carefully, ask yourself if there is neglected, untapped talent lying latent in your firm.

> On one of my consulting assignments in China, I was stranded in a remote area for two days while waiting for a charter flight. The flight had, unfortunately, developed engine trouble and was being repaired at its originating airport. For part of the second day, I had no laptop battery left, and my phone battery was down to less than 10%, so I sat under a tree, wrote a little bit in my notebook, and generally watched the ambling pace of life in the countryside. I watched a farmer building a wall out of stones. He wasn't using cement, so he was relying on the "fit" of the stones to generate his structural stability. He first spent a lot of time gathering stones, and he

placed them in three piles; larger angular stones, smaller angular stones and smoother or rounder stones of all sizes. Only after the piles were quite large did he begin with the wall. His selection of each stone was deliberate, and he chose painstakingly from each pile, sometimes testing the fit of a stone and then rejecting it for that placement, putting it back in the pile he had taken it from. As the piles diminished, he wandered off and began collecting stones again, until the piles were of a healthy size, and then he began stacking the wall once more. The second time he wandered off, I innocently sauntered over to his wall and looked at it more closely. It was packed tightly and looked surprisingly strong.

In my view, the Chinese farmer used the same type of foresight needed to build a good—or great—consulting firm. The piles of stones he collected represented the type of market intelligence needed to identify the pool of employees, and each pile represented a different type of consultant. His choice of placement began with a strong foundation, and every stone he placed in the wall added to or maintained that strength. If it didn't do either of those things, he put it back in the pile. He kept going back to the market and understanding what was available, preselecting his future stock. It might have taken him a bit longer to build that wall, but it wasn't going to give way under stress. It was a good wall.

In building a successful consulting practice—just like building a wall—you need to know your materials. You need to know what materials have special properties and are a little bit rare, and where they fit. You should be judicious, hiring carefully and therefore firing rarely. And, importantly, that reluctance to hire and that painstaking selection should be displayed by your senior staff when they hire people.

There is a common saying among consulting CEOs that illustrates the need to acknowledge this aspect of consulting. The saying is *resource for the lows, not the highs, in the workload.* The wisdom of this saying is that it encourages you to form your core team so that it is there all the time, in times of high workload and in low workload, directing and achieving exemplary client-focused outcomes. During the high-workload periods, you will need to take on more personnel, perhaps on short-term contracts, to manage the extra workload. These extra personnel are, temporarily, "filler" material. They are interchangeable resources, fulfilling specific tasks, and you will need to be reasonably objective and clinical—yet respectful—in how you manage this interchangeability. As your consulting firm grows, it is possible that you will have permanent "filler" material in your labor force. You will recognize them as interchangeable, and you will bow to market labor forces pragmatically with these, losing and gaining some in times of flux and competitive labor demand, a business-as-usual ebb and flow. But you will guard your potent hunters, farmers, creatives, and closers carefully, because you will recognize them as the essence of your success.

SOURCES OF CONSULTANTS

There are four common places that yield consultants for your firm. The first, and most obvious, is other consulting firms. These consultants are attractive candidates for three main reasons—they may already be known by clients, they may possess strong hunter or farmer attributes, and they are (hopefully) comfortable with the *ronin*-like life of a consultant. This last reason is not to be underestimated, because the other sources of consultants discussed in the following are sometimes prone to a change of heart about the challenges of consulting.

The second source of consulting is private industry. These consultants are often prized for their sector knowledge, their client contacts in the sector, and for their ability to move easily from one part of the private sector (industry) to another (consulting). Sector knowledge is a strategic advantage if it is current. All industries move through phases and cycles, and respond to technological and customer changes constantly. As a result, the insights that are applicable to individual sectors change continually. Remember, high-end consulting requires knowledge, analysis, and insight. Cutting-edge insights are powerful differentiators.

A third source is government. Government-sector candidates often come with deep knowledge and insights, but historically many have found the pace of working in government and in consulting to be quite different to each other. This is changing, as government departments increasingly borrow from the lessons of the private sector as they go through productivity reforms. As government bureaucracies change and work styles begin to mirror the private sector, there is less and less of a culture shock in the transition.

The fourth source is academia, where much innovation is fostered. Knowledge and analysis are developed in force in this sector, often at the leading edge, and the volume of "new" entrants into the marketplace each year is staggering. Graduates, graduate scholars, and researchers often bring with them fresh perspectives rather than experience, and can add depth to the consulting proposition of any firm. "They also come cheap," observes Colin, an economist we met in Chapter 1.

What trends do recruiters observe? First, consultants are largely drawn from a gene pool of consultants. The majority of people hired for mid- and senior-level consulting firms come from other consulting firms. This is because the traits of hunters and farmers are highly valued, and consulting is the only industry that visibly develops these. Second, a significant proportion of junior consultants hired come from academia and private industry. This is because both pools contain knowledge as well as analysis skills in large amounts. And third, appointments of government personnel into consulting roles were more noticeable at the senior strata of consulting. This is because governmental roles, especially at senior levels, often have strategy and broad stakeholder management skills.

Irrespective of where you draw your consultants from, you are investing in people. This investment is as much, if not more, important than in other industries because people comprise close to 100% of a consultancy's tangible assets. And it also because the strengths that people bring, in knowledge, analysis, and insight, are what your clients pay for. These strengths are best accessed when people are at their most engaged, and keeping people engage requires a great deal of investment in your culture. We discuss that more in Chapter 4.

Observe the growth of consulting firms, and you will notice from the résumés of people joining these firms at midlevel positions that they are largely consultants. Where do they all come from? Consulting has quite a high volume of staff that move from one consulting firm to another consulting firm. They move for the usual reasons; better positions, better projects, or better pay. They are also refugees from failed or faltering consultancies. In Chapter 1, we observed that the consulting landscape is littered with these. There are also many consultancies that grow too fast, resulting in the shedding of staff. In addition to this, because many in the private industry and public service see consulting as temporary stop on the way to another private industry or public service role, there are many transit employees in the market.

It is worth being aware of the characteristics of what is often a plentiful supply of consultants as you think about your sustainable growth plan. Teach yourself to look for the signs of career consultants; the ones who enjoy—as opposed to merely endure—the cut and thrust of the consulting world. When recruiting, be mindful of what you are looking for—knowledge, analysis, insight, and in what proportion. Categorize your choices—are they, or do they have the potential to be, creative-hunters, creative-farmers, closer-hunters, or closer-farmers? The more mindful you are of your choices, the more successfully you will build your foundation, and subsequently build upon it.

STARTING CONUNDRUM

When you start your firm, and you are everything from the secretary to the CEO, your employer brand is you, and you alone. People will not join you for your prestigious company name, although in some cases, if your professional reputation precedes you or you leave a firm in which you are highly respected by your employees, you may develop a following. There are only two key drawcards you have at this stage to attract employees—good pay and good projects. You do not have a structure within which to appoint senior people; you cannot easily sell to a prospective employee that you are offering a promotion from their previous role.

But it gets worse. At the start of your venture, your cash flow position may not allow you to attract people to your above-market salary or leveraged bonus scheme, which neutralizes one drawcard. And so you are left with good projects.

Every starting firm has this hurdle to get over. Your journey, in building and selling a successful consulting firm, does not begin at the time when you register your company and become a legal entity. At that point, you have made a consulting firm materialize (it is just you, the sole trader, or your group of partners), but it is just a vehicle. You may have consulting assignments that keep you busy and pay your salary, but your vehicle is simply parked on the side of the highway. It does not grow until you have ignition. And ignition is often the first assignment or assignments with which you can attract people and employ them for a fair market salary.

Failure to ignite is the most common reason that consulting firms do not grow beyond the starting point—whether it is you, a sole trader, or a group of partners. It is still a viable and lucrative business, but it does not grow.

All consultants trade on their personal brand, but at this point in time—preignition—you will need to trade as heavily as you ever will on your clients' perception of you. You will need your clients to give you more work than you can handle. And many clients are wary of overloading small consultancies with big—and therefore probably important—assignments. What if they don't have the capacity to complete the assignment? What if it takes too long to build the capacity given the time constraints of the assignment?

At this point, let us acknowledge that you can hire people and then seek assignments to feed your already grown firm. This is a jump-start, not ignition. It can achieve the same outcome as ignition, but it takes a lot more of your resources to achieve. If you can afford to do it, you may overcome client trepidation more readily than you might otherwise. It may be a good risk to take, but often it is not.

In Chapter 5, we discuss the mechanics of growth. A useful option for many starting firms is to work with other lone consultants, or other firms that provide body-shopping services. By being able to draw on these extra resources (at a premium cost), you can demonstrate to the client market that you can take on larger assignments and manage external resources to achieve the desired outcomes. You can do this while maintaining a consistent positive cash flow which, as we discuss in Chapter 6, is critical to the healthy function of your business. This builds your brand from "just me" to "my management ability." Once your personal brand is augmented by your success in managing larger projects by managing others, and clients consequently offer you projects that need two, three, or ten people to undertake, you will have the ability to hire staff rather than contract out smaller, discrete assignments. Then you have ignition.

If you are contemplating growing your own successful consulting firm, think about your ignition. Make sure you have a clear view about what that looks like, and your likelihood of achieving it. There are a great many consultants in the industry who have always wanted to grow a successful firm, but who have not carefully thought about their ignition source for growth. Like novice surfers, they jump into the water and wait, hopefully, for a big wave to surf in. They leave it to chance, rather than selecting their timing. The seasoned surfer prowls the coast looking for long, workable rides that match his or her ability. This surfer stands on headlands and looks at the wind, the waves and the riptides before deciding that this beach, and this time, is right. Be the seasoned surfer.

Sharon, a control-system engineer, explains how she started her consulting firm. "I was working in [a large consulting firm] during the early days of unconventional gas development. There was a lot of buzz about shale gas and how it could renew the US economy, and then government policy was introduced to stimulate this industry. I quit my job and began consulting in gas control systems. I knew several engineers who freelanced in small pipeline instrumentation so when I received a design-and-implement job I would do the design and have them do the installation, paying them daily rates. After a few months the work was steady so I hired one, then two of the freelancers. My profits started to grow and I was able to hire another designer, then two more installers, without much financial risk. It just developed from there."

Sharon's ignition point was the start of a new industry which had traditionally been supplied by larger consulting firms. As that industry grew, it created a demand in which she was able to leverage her design skills and instrumentation contacts to create rapid growth.

CHARACTERISTICS OF GOOD CONSULTANTS

Earlier in this book, we looked at the three attributes that make a good consultant—knowledge, analysis, and insight. Knowledge—the familiarity with subject matter—is relatively simple to spot. Your interviews will tell you whether the person has the required depth of knowledge to be a junior consultant, a senior consultant, or even a consultant at all. Similarly, the right questions during interviews will reveal whether the candidate has the analytical approach you are looking for. McKinsey's, the famous management consulting firm, is well-known for rejecting applicants on the basis that their thinking is not structured enough. Good interviewers use problem solving questions to probe a candidate's analytical abilities. Some consulting businesses—for example advertising—are less enamored by analytical abilities, and place a greater stock on insights. Insight is much harder to spot. Some successful recruiters claim they seek a "fuzzy logic" quality in consultants; one that makes a greater use of intuitive skills. Others depict this as the potential to take a "helicopter view" of the assignment, seeing things for perspectives that others, wrestling with knowledge and analysis, may often miss.

Roberto, one half of the leadership of a successful consulting practice, was searching for a senior practice leader. The consulting skills Roberto sought were in securing government approvals for infrastructure projects in different countries. The interview was a long and meandering affair. Roberto was affable, and he set the candidate at ease. His questions were open-ended, problem solving questions. Most started with "How would you …" or "Why did you ….?" I noticed that Roberto was checking knowledge and analysis dutifully (if a bit randomly), but was mostly searching for insight. After ninety minutes had passed it was evident that the candidate knew his stuff, and was a clear and structured thinker. Yet Roberto was not satisfied because he had not seen the insight he was looking for. He jumped up and pulled reports off his bookshelf, pointing out issues and debating them animatedly with the candidate. He very theatrically threw law books on the table to punctuate questions about due process. The interview was entertaining and the candidate was frequently arguing with Roberto, who was clearly goading the professional cut and thrust. And then, after a crescendo of debate, Roberto stopped. The room was silent for a few moments. He nodded, walked over to the seated candidate and thrust out his hand. "Well, I'm keen," he said with a big grin.

They talked terms and eventually the candidate agreed to take the role, later becoming a key member of the management team when the firm was sold some years later. I later asked Roberto if all of his interviews were that involved and challenging. He nodded. "I only interview for three or four roles a year, for key middle-level and senior positions, which turns out to be ten or twelve interviews of vetted candidates. By the time they get to me, we know they can do the job. Then I look for the X Factor, and I have a high rate of rejection so I usually only fill one or two of the roles. But I've yet to fill those roles with a dud."

FINDING CONSULTANTS

How do you find the consultants you need? Let us start with where your candidates might come from—government, academia, private industry, and another consulting firm (or they may be lone consultants). Naturally, while each candidate will be unique, there are some practical trends to be aware of.

Consultants from government or academia can bring with them knowledge and expertise, because these employees from these institutions are encouraged to be thorough, and are given the time to research and analyze with fewer time and budget pressures than in other sectors. Extracting consultants from government or academia can also be reasonably straightforward because consulting can be more financially rewarding than these institutions. Of course, financial rewards are not everything and not all government employees or academic experts are lured by the financial prospects of consulting, but it is a distinctive edge in your recruitment. However, commercial acumen, sales ability, and client stewardship are not often emphasized in these sectors. If you value these characteristics, examine your candidates from these sectors carefully.

The private industry sector, which holds many clients, is a fertile source of good consultants. In the private sector, competitive advantage is built on knowledge and execution, so candidates are schooled in extracting competitive advantage from knowledge. In addition, candidates often possess sector-specific insights, which adds tremendously to their ability to find competitive advantages. They are also generally used to time and budget pressures, which makes them relatively resilient to the often frenetic pace of consulting. Counterbalancing this is the fact that the private sector pays well. This means that the incentive you provide to attract successful private-sector professionals can be quite high.

From a practical statistical perspective, a reasonable percentage of your consulting firm might be drawn from experienced consultants. So let us spend a little bit of time on this. When recruiting from the consulting sector, it is worth recognizing that consulting is highly competitive. There are several reasons for this. The entry threshold is low. Anyone can become a consultant, which means there can be many consultants in a single professional and geographic catchment. Consultants compete for advisory services, which often have a smaller economic value than, say, building a house or buying a fleet of trucks. Because there are a lot of smaller-fee services required by clients, competition can be intense. Unlike the construction industry, in which there is a scale effect that reduces competition (e.g., a large construction firm is unlikely to bid for a contract to build the extension to your house), this effect is less evident in consulting. It is common to see a Big 4 consulting firm bid for the same work that a second- or third-tier company might bid for.

Such a competitive industry breeds competitive participants. In addition to competing for consulting contracts, consulting firms compete with each other for staff. And consultants are used to looking for bigger, brighter, and better outcomes in their problem-solving world, so they are as predisposed as—and perhaps even more so than—any other professional group to look around for better employment opportunities.

So the good news for you is that consultants are a reasonably mobile group of professionals. They move often. Large consulting firms know that it can be surprisingly easy to lose staff to the public or private industry sectors, or to other consulting firms. The question for you might be *what is it about your consulting firm that makes it attractive to consultants?*

Magda, a recruitment advisor, offers three attributes that attract good consultants to a firm. "They are—in order of merit—challenging assignments, leadership opportunity and success incentives on top of market salaries. Firstly, consultants know that the challenging assignments go to the firms that have that reputation with clients—that they can deliver the tough jobs. So that is a mark of reputation. Secondly, good consultants like to be at the top of the game, which usually includes leading the teams that take on the challenging assignments. And thirdly, consultants live risk and reward every day because their jobs are secure only if they are winning work and executing it well. So if they are beating the competition, they understand the value of that, and incentive schemes are expected. If you can offer all three of these, you can attract some of the best consultants from blue chip firms. If you can offer the first two, you'll still get them but be prepared to talk equity and shares. And if you can only offer the first one, you'll get the young up-and-comers, which is not a bad thing as your company matures."

CONSULTANTS WHO CAN SELL WORK

At this point, it is worth discussing consultants who can sell contracts. Many owners prize this quality highly. They often generously reward individuals who can sell; these supersellers are sometimes called "rainmakers." However, many smaller businesses fail in the early months and years because they invest too early in rainmakers without comparing the risk of this investment with the practical value carefully.

Take a look at recruiter advertisements for senior consultants. We often see a business development component in the advertisements, perhaps using the terms "leverage contacts" or "generate sales." When starting up your own consulting firm, you could be forgiven for thinking that this is a desirable, and even necessary, attribute to look for in your consultants. Of course there is no doubt this is useful quality; the ability to shepherd business to the door of your consulting firm. They are the hunters we discussed earlier in this chapter. But tread carefully. If these hunters are not endowed with knowledge, analysis, and insight—or at least two of those three—think carefully before hiring them. Consultants who cannot produce excellent consulting work rarely create lasting value, even in purely business development roles. Clients might initially join you because a business development consultant has brought them through your doors, but they will only come back to seek those consultants who have knowledge, analysis, and insight. They will bypass the salesperson. The business development consultant's value proposition then becomes finding new clients. This is a good value proposition if, for example, you have carefully segmented your market, you are taking a run at a new segment, and your business development professional is familiar with and has good client contacts in that segment. But it is a risky proposition if you hire a business development professional—who does not perform as a good consultant—simply because you want more sales.

At the beginning of your consulting enterprise, hiring a salesperson who cannot undertake excellent consulting is a salary cost that may be hard to justify. On the other hand, larger companies use business development consultants well, particularly when seeking large projects that subsequently utilize dozens or even hundreds of consultants for longer periods of time. The scale leverage works in those circumstances because the business owner or executive team is able to pay the business development consultant's salary and costs from a percentage of the profits created by the volume of consulting work brought in and carried out. In smaller firms, this subsidy model often works much less effectively because the scale leverage required to operate profitably (the number of fee-earning consultants per business development consultant) is too small.

CREATING AN ENGAGING WORKPLACE

An engaging workplace improves productivity. People who like working where they are employed produce their best work. Your job, as a leader, is to make that happen. Not just because it is a good thing to do, but also because it gives your firm a considerable competitive advantage. While this engaging environment is important in most types of work, there are very few professions for which this is more important than in consulting. The reason, of course, is that you are harnessing bright minds to deliver top quality service, and you will get neither the creative brilliance nor the service mentality you need if your staff are not engaged.

There is no magic formula for creating an engaging workplace, but much of it has to do with your leadership. If you let engaging behaviors happen, they are more likely to become the norm. If you let disengaging behaviors happen, then they are more likely to repeat and become embedded. If your behaviors are engaging or disengaging, expect to have your choice reflected back at you. From the start, what you do or don't do will shape how engaged your workplace is.

Most consulting leaders who started their firm confess to underestimating the amount of time, outside of their "day job" of client stewardship, winning work, quality control, service delivery, and running a firm, was required to create an engaging workplace.

A growing environmental firm in Canada began to think about its engagement about a year or so after it was created. The owner, Helen, who was in her 40s and had no children, was a serious person who worked long hours and had immense professional pride. She did not enjoy socializing too much and, in her own words, was not "a magnetic leader." However, understanding the value of an engaging workplace, she tried to be more definitive about what that might mean for her staff. It was becoming clear to Helen that her focus on creative solutions to unique problems fit a certain age demographic. Employees with 8 to 15 years' experience had agile minds, they had not become set in their ways, and they were hungry for fame and success. They were also getting married or having babies.

So Helen decided to become much more family friendly. She did not want to lose the edge that she had, which was a powerful work ethic; one that had served her well. She decided to combine the family-friendly platform with a work hard, play hard culture. She instituted work-from-home programs with some investment in digital technology, and struck a deal with a commercial crèche center within walking distance of her largest office to give her staff discounted child care services. In two steps, she created a flexible work environment that acknowledged the importance of family life to her staff, despite the fact that she, by her own admission, was not a family-oriented person.

She remarked that by the time a year had passed, she could see a difference. Creative output was up. Productivity was up. Client satisfaction was up. She really liked the culture that emerged, and noted that it was energized from within. Tight-knit offices were formed, and there was a slight edge of elitism, which is distinctly not a liability in a consulting firm. Successes were celebrated and failures were despised for the palpable embarrassment they created. If her firm lost a prospect, she would be philosophical about it, but she reported that her staff seemed to take it more personally.

"It was like having over-achieving children," she said. "The family-friendly work-hard ethic seemed to make people more fiercely protective of their success. It was as if they wanted the model to work for me, because it worked for them personally."

Helen noticed that staff who benefited from this arrangement seemed more engaged because they had a better work-life balance. They simply worked with more enthusiasm, which in turn led to better consulting outcomes. Staff that did not directly benefit from this arrangement saw what was being done, and felt the effects in a more vibrant workplace, many commenting to her and others that the company had a "nice culture."

Livingstone, who owns a firm that consults in human capital and productivity, grew his practice in South Africa after Nelson Mandela implemented Black Economic Empowerment (BEE) policies. He says an engaging workplace is made up of many "small attributes" that create a halo effect. "The effect is more engaging in smaller or midsized firms if the leader is seen to be investing thought, time and effort in personally ensuring these small attributes come to life. The value of the engagement is then made up of three things: the attribute you implement that positively affects some, the way others who are not directly affected become complicit in the higher engagement, and the visible personal investment of the leader in making the attribute happen. And then it matters less about what attributes you choose, as long as they are valuable to some, and more about how often and how authentically you implement those attributes. So it can be encouraging thought diversity, or innovation, or discouraging gender bias or ethnic bias … it depends on what is valuable to your people and your business culture."

Many things go toward making a workplace engaging. The basic needs of a functioning organization must, of course, be met—getting paid on time (and accurately!), tax and superannuation compliance, information technology that works, lighting and climate control, and so on. Without the basics, all other forms of engagement have a much reduced likelihood of being successful.

Many smaller businesses claim they cultivate an open culture through a relatively flat structure, with flexible rules and regulations. The theory here is that, by being the opposite of larger corporations, an engaging workplace is cultivated. This can be engaging to some but less engaging to others; it is largely an issue of personal preference. The lack of bureaucracy and rules does not necessarily translate to an engaging workplace. There are many examples of hierarchical, rules-based workplaces that score very highly on engagement. Beware the trap of assuming that simply because you have a small-to-medium–sized business, your firm is somehow charming and engaging. Creating an engaging workplace takes more effort than that.

Leadership, clearly, sets the tone for engagement. A leader who walks around frequently and talks to staff can be very engaging, although it becomes less practical to do this at a meaningful frequency as your firm grows larger, or gets spread out over a diverse geography. Yet it should be noted that many introverted leaders who are not known for their management by walking around style have created engaging leadership styles, so don't despair if you are not an extrovert. The garrulous consulting leader is entertaining, yes, but not necessarily pivotal to an engaging workplace.

As a leader, your most powerful tool is implementing genuine, lived policies that make people feel safe and valued. If you have policies that genuinely cultivate and celebrate characteristics that contribute to these feelings of being safe and valued, people are engaged. In consulting, you want your hunters, farmers, creatives, and closers to each feel safe and valued for what they bring to your firm. The policies need not be formal as much as they need to be consistently lived, but writing them down and ensuring that they have visibility in your firm will not hurt.

Karl, a conflict resolution consultant in Switzerland, argues that the most engaging policies are the ones written by staff. "After we had grown to about 20 people, we decided we needed more formal policies that would help define our culture. So we asked our people to develop a charter of how we would work. We called it The Way We Work. From that charter we developed policies that would guide existing and future new staff behaviors to deliver on The Way We Work. The charter has words like 'trust' and 'openness' and 'service', and then we have policies with intriguing names like Open Door, Client Return and Safe Dissent that spell out how we interact. There are 18 policies in total that shape our engagement culture."

Beyond behavioral policies, which build engagement through the way people interact at work, there are policies that acknowledge that people work to live, and not the other way around. Policies that create a better work-life balance extend the feeling of safety and value beyond employees and into their families and friends. Helen, whom we met earlier in this chapter, implemented family-friendly policies that made her employees' spouses and children feel safe and valued. The extension of this zone of safety and value into employees' families is a strong "stay" attribute. Research on motivators for joining a company and leaving a company shows that the decision to join a company is largely owned by the employee, with family input largely centered around relocation and commuting issues. Conversely, the decision to leave a company or to stay is much more likely to be influenced by family input. Spouses who feel that the company policies benefit the employee's household are much more likely to encourage their partners to find ways to stay with a company. Helen, in her environmental firm, agrees. "My best employees get headhunted frequently, and a lot of the time the offering is more money. But I find that, most of the time, we have discussions about what it will take for people to stay, rather than receiving a surprising notice of resignation. And I have yet to need to outbid a headhunter because the sense I get is that my employees want to stay, with some adjustments—to salary, to career prospects, to work arrangements that further improve broader family life ... you know, more than just money, particularly in that 35 to 50 age group, where I have some of my best consultants. There is a reluctance to leave, and that reluctance seems to be the reason I keep my staff for as long as I do."

Policies that are set to engage, but which are not supported by employees' lived experience, actually have a more disengaging effect than no policies at all. The reason, explains New York-based organizational psychologist Vikram, is a sense that the firm, or the leader, is disingenuous—which in turn erodes safety. "If you have a policy and you unflinchingly enforce it, you have strong rules and boundaries ... and they are real and consistent, so you have safety. If you have no policy, you have ambiguity, which is sort of a neutral zone. But if you have a policy and you don't enforce it, employees see this as a form of organizational lying, and you have an unsafe environment. So the lesson there is, policies set to build a certain culture are good, but only if you really mean it. If you don't, you are better off not having those policies."

Many smaller consulting firms adopt policies that their clients have, because it feels "professional" to do so. While it is true that formalizing policies is a professional approach, a larger corporation might have these policies in place for much different reasons than you might. For example, a large client firm might have a gender pay equality policy that requires progressive reductions in gender pay gaps (typically, reducing and eliminating the trend that men get paid more than women in equivalent roles).

For a large firm, with a statistically significant population of both men and women, any pay gap is likely to persist because there is a systematic problem. If there is a systematic problem, and the large firm is a high-profile listed company, there may be external pressure to eliminate the problem. There may be pressure to report publicly on the gender pay outcomes. But your firm might not have these pressures, leaving you with the moral obligation, rather than the reputation pressure, to ensure gender pay equity. Recognizing this, you may or may not elect to have a formal gender pay equality policy, although you might in practice be vigilant and have open conversations to ensure that gender pay inequalities are avoided.

> Paolo, one half of a very successful multinational enterprise, recalls a failed safety policy that was instituted at his firm. "We worked for major industrials, who used sophisticated systems such as DuPont's safety system. So we formalized our overarching safety policy, which was a good thing. But we also formalized a number of policies, including detailed hazard assessment policies and strict travel safety policies that required trip evaluations. In reality, our staff were rarely in hazardous situations and these policies soon became painful to use every day. So we had these policies, but we started turning a blind eye to them. A year later, we were getting consistent feedback that management was not serious about safety. So we re-worked the policies, deliberately avoiding the DuPont-type sophistication, and made them much simpler. Our safety performance actually improved, and 2 years later our employee feedback was that management valued employee safety. In reality, absolutely nothing had changed in our commitment. Our over-enthusiastic adoption of sophisticated policies that our clients valued, but that we didn't need, created a problem for us."

Policies, therefore, set the framework of an engaged workplace, and action—in particular yours, as the leader—fills in that framework with the substance that helps deliver an engaged workplace. Many larger companies apply a model of employee engagement that attempts to get the best out of employees by configuring the workplace appropriately, and this model is particularly useful for consulting firms. This model depends on matching an attractive culture that you set via expectations, policies, and systems, with the lived experiences of your staff. A measure of the level of engagement of your people, they argue, depends on how much they praise your firm to others; how difficult it would be for them to leave; and how inclined they are to produce their personal best within your firm. These three attributes amount to, respectively, a greater attractiveness to good consultants to join you; low staff turnover rates and the corresponding enrichment of your succession strategy that in turn allows you to avoid the golden handcuff at exit; and attain top shelf consulting outcomes for your clients.

But it doesn't stop there in consulting, asserts Zhou, a consultant in manufacturing efficiency in Shanghai who leads a midsized firm with several offices across China. "Consultants look up to good consultants. I find that I must work hard to stay at the top of my own game in order for my staff to feel like they have a leader they can follow. It is tempting to spend too much time on administrative affairs and neglect consulting skills. I am mindful all the time that if I myself do not have something unique to offer as a consultant, my leadership ability suffers." Most consultants agree with this. If the CEO of a consulting firm is not an astute, accomplished, and currently effective consultant, the attractiveness of that firm diminishes.

"In big firms," says Rachel, a veteran of 10 years' consulting, "the Chief Executive and Board are out of sight, so you look to the Principal Consultants for that role modeling. But in a smaller firm, the owner or Chief Executive is quite visible, and if that person isn't a consultant that I would aspire to be, I find my enthusiasm fades."

In addition to the leadership-led culture, there is also the team-based culture that is cocreated by your staff. All of the above can be neutralized by a poor team-based culture. There are two aspects to team-based culture; a performance-oriented aspect and a workplace-oriented aspect.

The performance-oriented aspect attempts to connect individual excellence with group excellence, creating a shared performance that leverages individual performance. Such a culture encourages some competitiveness between your staff (e.g., the bonus structure for client satisfaction, or sales, or repeat client work, or innovative outcomes) but does not allow the competition to become combative. Win–win competitiveness in the operating culture is healthier, more productive, more profitable, and more stable than win–lose competitiveness. Smart leaders understand the value of shared goals and shared rewards, while appreciating the leveraged value of individual goals and rewards that do not undermine the former.

What does that balance look like? Many successful firms apportion a specific percentage of profit to the bonus pool and divide that bonus pool into two parts; one for shared goals and rewards, and one for individual goals and rewards. The balance between the two is highly dependent on the firm's structure, the number of people, and the preset key performance indicators. It is not unusual for firms to report anything from a shared to individual bonus pool ratio of 30:70 through 50:50 through to 70:30. Many firms have balanced scorecards, where shared goals, individual goals or both have financial and nonfinancial criteria attached to them.

The workplace-oriented aspect of a team-based culture is all about the "feel" of your firm. If that sounds vague, that is because it is. The "feel" of one firm will not appeal to some, but will appeal to others. But it is not about the attractiveness to outsiders; it is about the attractiveness to those within the firm, its "stay" appeal. That "stay" appeal, according to organizational psychologists like Vikram, is created by those within the firm who want to make a "professional home." If successful, he asserts, it can also be a powerful attractor of others outside the firm who are like-minded—but its intention is subconsciously biased toward those already within the firm.

> "It is a social setting," he explains. "This can be the collegiate atmosphere. It can be about the coffee machine or the lunch area, or the after-work sports or barbecues, or bringing your kids to work. It can be about the pool table or XBox room or the library. It can be the charities, the Fun Runs, the volunteering at the shelters. This space is virtually limitless and wide open to your creativity. By allowing some of these activities to flourish, you create the space for people to invest something personal around their workplace. Those individual investments combine to create a social environment. The social environment, in turn, is like glue in your culture. It binds people. And you evolve—from just a professional organization into a social, professional organization."
>
> Zhou puts it another way. "People work together in average ways if they merely coexist. But if they feel they belong together, they work better. So an engaged workplace is often one where the feeling is one of comradeship or family. That is why some small businesses seem to be so effective; because the employees are more connected to each other, there is loyalty to one another and there is loyalty to their business."

Sadly, many consulting firms use a simple labor multiplier model and find that their growth becomes limited to 5, 10, or 20 people as a result. This is because they are simply working a formula, which is to pay a fixed salary of x, and create an income stream of 1.5 times x or 2 times x for each person. This is a profitable enterprise, but the strategy is a limiting one. Successful consulting businesses recognize that this labor multiplier model is simply an outcome of a deeper strategy. That deeper strategy is finding and keeping great consultants; hunters, farmers, creatives, and closers in the right mix that are engaged, that consolidate and grow your business, that create inherent value in the firm, and that provide you with an elegant Exit Strategy.

THREE TIPS

Tip 1: Never forget that consulting is a service industry. That means you, and your consultants, need to ensure that both your delivery and the process of achieving your delivery meet or exceed client expectations.

Tip 2: Think about your consultants strategically. Understand what different types of consultants you need, and build your talent pool carefully, using that understanding. Hire with great thought about what you need in your firm at your exit.

Tip 3: An engaged workplace will enhance creativity, client stewardship, and delivery of assignments. Think about the culture you want to create, the tools for building engagement, and how you will engage and retain your good consultants.

4

Building Your Firm

Choose a job you love and you will never have to work a day in your life.

Confucius

YOUR FIRM'S BUILDING BLOCKS

One of the benefits of starting your own consulting firm is that you can do what you want. And one of the dangers of starting your own consulting firm is that you can do what you want. It's a volatile paradox; one that can blow up in your face. The freedom you have in doing what you want can erode the discipline you need to do what you have to, to meet your Exit Strategy.

If you are a lone consultant, a one-person band, you can play exactly to your strengths. In fact, if there is a good market for your strengths (e.g., if the demand exceeds the supply), playing to your strengths can be very profitable. Your fee rate or charge-out rate is directly proportional to the degree of difficulty of the specialized area you work in, and your expertise in that area. So if you do complicated work that few people can do, you can hold your charge-out rate at a high level. On the other hand, if you do simpler work that many people can do, your charge-out rate will tend to be lower.

A rule of thumb is that you'll work less, for more money, if you can sustainably hold your charge-out rate at a high level. And ideally, you'll turn down projects because you're too busy, the projects don't turn you on or frankly, you prefer to be sipping Mai Tais on a beach in Spain between June and August every year, and—what the hell—do the same in the southern hemisphere around December and January. This sweet spot is not something you'll encounter all the time, but it is not rare either. And when you do find a sweet spot, often markets work to rub out the sweet spot.

It works like this: If you provide a rare consulting service for which the demand exceeds the supply, you will charge high rates and profit from it, but you will not be able to meet market demand. Now, because there are relatively low barriers to entering a consulting market, the unmet need will attract a number of contenders, in the form of other consulting firms. Unless your work comprises a specialized intellectual property that only you own, the market eventually corrects (and often overcorrects). This happens in the form of supply meeting or exceeding demand. When the latter happens, charge-out rates or total fees start to reduce, in real terms, because of the increasingly competitive nature of the work. The sweet spot reduces, and eventually fades into the background of consulting services.

If you're building your consulting empire, it's even harder to find that sweet spot, let alone keep it for a while. Many factors interfere with your prospects. Labor limitations are the most significant factor. It works much like a bigger version of the previous example, where the sweet spot disappears. If you're famous for your skills at doing a particular type of consulting job—let's call it heroic consulting—you will be in demand. So you hang out your shingle for heroic consulting and you go looking for other heroic consultants to recruit into your band of entrepreneurs. Quite soon you discover there aren't many of these heroic consultants around. If there were, they would be doing much the same as you are, and they wouldn't be working for you; they would be working for themselves. But you persist with hiring and training staff in heroic consulting. You're growing to meet the demand in heroic consulting.

But, as you grow to meet demand, the market then starts to correct, with a growth in heroic consulting supply. Some of these heroic consultants work for themselves, and others work in the bigger companies. If, after a while, there are lots of these heroic consultants around, then supply would be meeting demand, the niche fades away and eventually it ceases to exist.

So the concept that you can build a company of 100 people in heroic consulting is theoretically feasible, but in practice it mostly fails after a short time in the real world. Of course, the concept *sometimes* succeeds, but not that often. Typically, lack of diversification limits growth potential.

So let's look at the "build" of consulting firms.

The smallest unit of consulting is the one-person band or the lone consultant.

One step up from the one-person-band model is the small-niche band. The small-niche band brings together a cadre of three, four, or five understudies in heroic consulting and, under your tutelage, forms into a potent small-niche consulting firm. If you are in a good market setting, your cadre might be 15 or 20 people, which is still a small-niche firm. You're still a long way off from your dreams of a consulting empire, but you have evolved from one person to a multiple of people, which is a pretty significant step up the evolutionary chain of consulting. You sense there is a domino effect that you can tap into.

Recall in Chapter 2, "The Exit Strategy," the concept of "cells" was mentioned. A cell is effectively a small-niche consulting firm. The very simple model of growth is to create a firm with a number of cells, or a number of these small-niche consulting units.

A key catalyst for growth is to find cells that are complementary to each other. Complementary cells are those that do not work in isolation. They sit on some kind of value chain and "knit" together to retain their individual value but still form part of a greater value bundle.

This requires a considerable amount of thinking and planning. I won't pretend it's easy or quick. The market is a moving, living ocean of opportunity. It is a tide of unfulfilled demand and eventual oversupply. Because we live in a world of increasing complexity, this tide is ever-changing. Because the consulting world has such low entry barriers, this tide moves quickly, and competitive advantages can be short lived.

So don't stop working, and reworking, your cell model. Don't stop, even after your months of planning have resulted in something that looks achievable, not even while you're achieving it 3 years later, not even when it looks like you have achieved it 6 years later. Every cell you add to this value chain of small-niche bands integrates overall value into your company.

Now, you're a consultant at heart. Which means you love doing work that is stimulating, and you'll get bored doing work that doesn't offer you the level of challenge and excitement that you crave. And while you can indulge that dislike of the less exciting work if you're a successful one-person band, be wary of allowing that freedom to translate to your bigger, more diverse, firm. If you want to enjoy absolutely everything the company does, you might feel like avoiding the "boring" or "unsexy" work, and you may balk at recruiting for the skills that are required to do that work. And if you choose to indulge this whim, you make your job much more complex. Remember the Chinese farmer and my kung fu experience? You need small round stones and big craggy stones to make a strong wall. Not all of the stones have eye-catching shapes and sizes.

Consultants will often talk about "bread-and-butter" work. This is everyday work. Not every problem is a unique problem. Not every consulting task requires exquisite knowledge and insight. A great deal of work on offer is reasonably straightforward work, which any good consultant with the requisite knowledge can do. This work—the bread-and-butter work—will underpin your steady cash flow, a very important aspect of your business that we will focus on in Chapter 6.

So your job in knitting together your cells is not to exclusively focus on the cutting-edge services and skills, but to supplement them with enough of the everyday services and skills to stabilize your company and to stabilize your cash flow. This is a complex task, certainly, but the good news is that there is no one single correct mix. There are many combinations of successful mixes.

There is an often-unsung benefit to getting your portfolio of small-niche-bands right, and it is organizational resilience. Industry seems to operate in cycles. There are boom times and slow times. International markets change the prospects of bigger clients, and national economies vary the prospects of smaller clients. Your clients' prospects affect yours, and quite directly. In some years, by mirroring changes to the industrial landscape around you, a handful of your cells will prosper while others might struggle. In other years, other cells prosper while previously lucrative cells might struggle. And while you might optimistically hope that none of your cells will ever struggle, to borrow a wise phrase, *hope for the best and plan for the worst.* Think of your portfolio of small-niche bands as a diversified strategy in motion. The diversification potentially makes you more resilient to the fickleness of markets.

In the following two diagrams, we use real revenue data from 5 years of consulting in a start-up office which grows, over 30 months, to a four-cell practice. The first cell was an auditing function, which displayed typical seasonal variability.

If we look at this single cell and assume that the growth did not happen, this is how susceptible the office is to market forces (Figure 4.1). The lumpy line shows the monthly consulting revenues, while the dotted line shows its long-term average.

A simple rule of thumb for measuring your susceptibility is to compare the range of the monthly income with a longer-term average income. In Figure 4.1, the range of monthly income is between $27,000 and $41,000, which is $14,000. The long-term average is $34,000. The ratio of the revenue

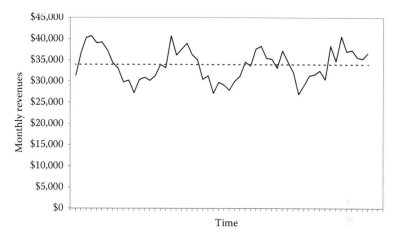

FIGURE 4.1
Single cell revenue fluctuations.

range to the average revenue is $14,000 divided by $34,000, or around 0.41, which is not a ratio that you would be confident running your business at.

The office then grew steadily to four cells. With four cells, the susceptibility to market forces can change in one of two ways. If the four cells are subject to the same ups and downs of the market, then there is a bigger boom-and-bust risk. However, if the cells are chosen well, the firm's revenues start to become less "lumpy" in relative terms while, of course, increasing. This is shown in Figure 4.2, which illustrates the revenue fluctuations in each of the four cells, and the resulting (relatively smaller) fluctuation in the firm's revenue. The dotted line following the total monthly revenue line is a moving 3-month average. The ratio, in Figure 4.2, of the monthly revenue range to the long-term monthly average is $38,000 divided by $141,000, or 0.27; which is significantly healthier than 0.41.

As the number of cells increases, the total revenue increases and, while revenue fluctuations remain, these fluctuations become less and less material relative to your moving average—provided your cells are not overly codependent on each other or overly dependent on the same market forces.

Does this always work in practice? Like most things in life, the answer is not "yes" or "no," but "more yes than no." The reason that it's not an unqualified "yes" is that you would have to be able to see the future of the market economies and operating models of your clients to get that answer. And if you could, you wouldn't start a consulting firm, you would play the stock market from your smartphone on a beach in the Seychelles.

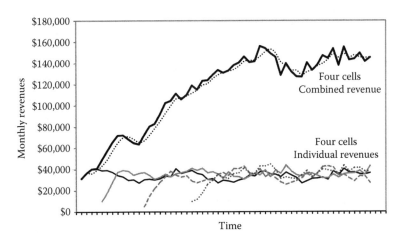

FIGURE 4.2
Multiple cell revenue fluctuations and resilience.

Given yours and my frustrating incompetence in reading the future accurately, the trick is putting knowledge into practice so that the answer does actually turn out to be "more yes than no."

Remember, the market fluctuations that occur and influence industries around you are outside of your control. You can only watch and marvel at boom-and-bust cycles. But the market fluctuations, and their influence on the industries around you, are not out of reach of your *understanding*. If you understand, for example, that oil price fluctuations affect some clients much more than they do others, your diversified strategy can build some resilience against a downturn in oil prices. If you know that some clients' successes are linked to each other (e.g., mining and manufacturing) but other clients are much less linked (e.g., agriculture and pharmaceuticals), you can assess your diversification strategy more thoughtfully. But it is not all about demand-side turbulence. Smart entrepreneurs saw, for example, the surge in IT consulting demand in the 1990s, but also understood that undersupply would soon turn to oversupply as the market for IT consultants overcorrected. A particularly clever entrepreneur I once met built his company out of IT cells and HR cells, creating a lucrative business, eventually, in human resource information systems, eventually cornering a very sustainable market of medium-sized clients who had to move from manual to IT-platform-based human resource management systems.

As you can see, the world of selecting and connecting your cells is a large, complex, and dynamic one. This world is full of innovative opportunities and resilience strategies. Think of the most comprehensive Lego set you have ever seen, filled with a plethora of sizes and shapes, and covering every primary and hybrid color you can imagine. Out of this vast Lego set, you have to pick a few that connect together to make an innovative, stable, and resilient shape. That is your role as the architect of your own firm. To constantly wade through the infinite Lego set and pick the pieces, then connect them together. You can be very adaptive, adding pieces that fit as the circumstances around you change.

Many entrepreneurs talk about supply synergy and value chain propositions. Supply synergy simply creates more than the sum of its parts in two different consulting propositions by enhancing each other in the market. Paired consulting examples are the aforementioned IT and human resources; environment and engineering; finance and law; event planning and photography. Of course, you will probably have more than two cells, so you will be looking for more complex synergies that work in your client context. Value chain propositions are more target-client focused. For example, if your target client is the food industry, then your value chain might extend from agriculture through to retail regulations. You may have consultants who are agronomists, economists, logistics, and specialists in consumer law. Rather than provide a single service, you might find points of value in the agricultural sector chain. If your target is development in the resources sector (e.g., mining, oil, or gas) then you might have consultants who specialize in gaining legal rights to resources, consultants who negotiate land access, consultants who run environmental and social impact assessments, and consultants who manage government relations with resource ministries. Clearly, the value chain proposition does create a greater dependency on the sectors that your firm relies upon for success, and that is a risk that you should evaluate carefully.

So you get the idea. Making your answer to the question "do cells work in practice?" more yes than no is an analytical process to which you should apply your innovation and market insight. You are an entrepreneur, so be imaginative. You don't need to follow others' models (but do learn from them!). You can tailor your cell strategy to suit your view of the markets in which you are operating.

To really evaluate your cell strategy, you should then step away from your proposed collection of Lego pieces, and look at what you have from a market perspective. Look at supply of each cell in the market, and then look at the demand for each cell. If demand exceeds supply, how high are the barriers to entry for new suppliers of cells like yours? Where in the market cycle are you?

Look at supply synergy carefully. Are you creating some unique synergies, and is there a sustainable demand for the synergies? Look at competitors that have some of your cells. Can the competitors also create the same synergies and flood your market, creating a commodity out of what you hoped was a unique differentiator? In your value chain propositions, are the client sectors upon whom you rely an upward trend, a downward trend, or are they stable? If they are stable, are they susceptible to downturns?

Look then at the combination of cells you have in place, and the combination that you are growing. Are they, in their aggregate, able to withstand market fluctuations? Will some carry others in downturns? Do you have any weaknesses, too many eggs in a single basket? Are your talented staff well distributed across your cells, and do you have staff that can move from one cell to the next during market fluctuations so that you can control your labor costs but still retain service quality?

So your architecture is vitally important. You want a combination of cells that gives you resilience to external forces, and internal nimbleness and flexibility. You want the cells to have some synergies in the market, and perhaps some integration across clients' value chains. You want to have your cell-by-cell view for demand and supply separately, together, for your clusters of cells, and for your whole organization. And you want to constantly update and refresh that view as you move from inception toward your Exit Strategy.

CONNECTING SECTORS AND SERVICES

Large consulting firms often model their activities around two axes. One axis is "services," which is essentially supply. The other is "sectors," which is where your demand comes from. Services are, as the name suggests, consulting services that are provided. Sectors are the industry segments that buy these services, like mining, pharmaceutical, defense, retail, manufacturing, oil and gas, telecommunications and so on.

This intersection of services and sectors is your accessed market. You can grow your market along these two axes.

If you have a cell that provides a service to a sector, and you are able to service a market demand in that sector, your growth question should be "what other sectors can this cell service?" Other client sectors might use the same service, and you leverage good service performance in one sector to sell the service into another sector. As you become successful, your cell grows. Then, your challenge is to maintain a profitable supply that does not outstrip demand; in other words, be careful that you do not grow that cell too much.

The other axis of growth is leveraging good client relationships to sell other services—other cells you may have—into the same client organization.

A services-and-sectors model is quite powerful in achieving cross-marketing growth across both axes. Now, rather than thinking about client organizations, consider client sectors and expand the scale of this model. The key to expanding the model of this scale is to understand if, why and how different companies in a single client sector recognize and transmit your service delivery reputation to each other.

The cross-marketing approach does two things at the sector scale. First, it sells multiple services into a single client sector. If your brand name is well respected by, say, several clients in the banking industry, you attempt to create more revenue from that industry by supplying other services to it, essentially leveraging off your reputation and goodwill. Often, your service level is key to selling multiple services in a client organization or a client sector. If the experience of how you do the thing that you do is well regarded (your service level), cross marketing within a sector becomes easier. Why? Because the people in one client sector network with each other far more than people across multiple sectors do. And if your firm is well regarded by, for example, telecommunications companies A and B, word of mouth will allow you to convert that goodwill to an entrée into telecommunications company C.

The cross-marketing approach builds a reputation for a particular service offering in that sector. There is a critical mass where, if you repeatedly and with consistently high quality provide a particular service to a client sector, your firm becomes well recognized for that service offering irrespective of the client sector. Your firm can use this recognition of excellence to break into new sectors in which the service carries value. So you become known for excellence in a service that had applications in Sector 1, and this excellence becomes your entrée to Sector 2.

Of course, these two axes of growth are self-evident. Your growth strategy comes not from recognizing what is reasonably obvious, but from creating a systematic strategy of growth along both axes simultaneously, or in tandem, or indeed in any kind of sequence that gives you a strategic advantage. At the start of your enterprise, your strategy is relatively simple, like a single or dual-celled organism that grows in somewhat predictable ways. But as your enterprise grows, and you have multiple cells providing multiple services to multiple sectors, the choices you make become increasingly strategic and have the potential to add tremendous value to your organization. Thinking along the two axes systematically helps to distill clarity from your complex and busy marketplace. In the next chapter, as we explore growth models, applying clear thinking across both axes becomes not just useful and value-adding, but necessary to manage your growth risk.

Consulting firms often start quite modestly, sometimes with only one service offering to just one client. This is the most basic of subsistence consulting, and it obviously comes with great risk. If your client has a downturn or has a budget cut, you feel it acutely. So most budding consulting firms take the next, logical risk-mitigation and revenue-enhancing step of applying their single service offering to other clients. And most consulting firms naturally have better success with other clients in the same sector as the first client because of the advantage of specific experience and sector familiarity. Both are comforting to client and consultant alike.

As the architect of your own firm, it is useful to understand two or three sectors intimately. I reason that if I can understand a couple of sectors well, I might gain some insights into the most useful collection of services around which I could build small-niche bands that appeal to multiple sectors, thus turbocharging my revenue engine.

Which sectors you pick will really depend on how ambitious you are. Aspirations of international or global growth may steer you toward sectors that are populated by multinational companies, which is a smaller choice of sectors than if you did not have international aspirations. Examples of sectors with international sector appeal include oil and gas, mining, food, manufacturing, and telecommunications. Other sectors, which may not lend themselves as well toward international growth, are, for example, the dairy industry, local government, quarrying, fishing, and mainstream tourism.

PROJECTING RESILIENCE

When you're striving for "more yes than no" in your strategy, your personal ability to handle the "no" moments is critical. These moments will happen, no matter how well formed your strategy is, and no matter how well you execute it. Markets are bumpy rides, growth aspirations are a dynamic, spring-loaded seat, and your resilient seatbelt is essential. For a growing company with you at the helm, your personal resilience correlates very strongly to business resilience.

Your personal resilience is important because in a small company you are the focal point. All eyes are on you. You're the satellite dish that transmits through word and deed (as well as the absence or insufficient amount of either), the governing "vibe" of the organization. The vibe you project is amplified, quite alarmingly, through the words and actions of the majority of your staff. Your cues become their cues, your frowns become their frowns, your personal black thundercloud becomes their collective supercell.

Words or actions that you think are innocuous can get beamed back at you, weeks or months later, at many times the wattage. If you project despair, you'll reap panic. If you meet challenges with confident determination, you'll see the same—and more—back from your staff. Small enterprises have an uncanny ability to mold themselves in your image.

Surprisingly, very few entrepreneurial leaders see this. In a world where, in recent times, being authentic has been hailed as the new leadership mantra, the value of stoic resilience in the face of adversity has been forgotten. Yet it remains a formidable weapon in your arsenal when you know that something will go wrong. There will be more "yes than no," but there will still be moments of "no." Starting your enterprise knowing this with certainty avoids two potential failures. One, of course, is the failure of naivety. Expecting everything to go your way is wonderfully optimistic, but it can be a shock to your system when the inevitable happens and something does not go your own way. The other potential failure is responding to the "no" moments in a negative way; one that becomes viral in your company and depletes morale rapidly.

Stoic resilience is not the absence or loss of authenticity. Rather, it is the presence of discipline and clear thinking. Even if your inner voice is saying *oh shit* while your cash flow is taking a turn for the worse, a quick internal acknowledgment that shit is, indeed, hitting a fast-revolving fan is all that is required. An external acknowledgment is not necessary, nor is it productive. Instead, work quietly and determinedly on your recovery.

Personal resilience is what you want from your pilot as your flight navigates dark thunderclouds and fuel is running low. That is exactly what your staff expect, and deserve, from you. Only you know that there is "more yes than no." Your staff should see maximum "yes" and, ideally, zero "no."

BEING MORE RIGHT THAN WRONG

In your enterprise, the selection of small-niche-band skills—the building blocks of your company—may not be preplanned all the way to the Exit Strategy, and to the actual exit. There is a great deal of adaptive behavior within your strategy.

The start is relatively straightforward. You play to your specific strengths. You have a set of small-niche-band skills; perhaps only one, even. You select perhaps two, three, or four sectors that you soon come to know reasonably well as you invest in knowledge about your broader market, and identify those parts of the market that support your broad vision.

You ensure you understand your chosen sectors' value chains, their general market economics, and the supply-and-demand mechanics of the commodities they deliver. You begin to understand how these sectors are structured—or more precisely, the range of conventional and unconventional management structures that these industries adopt. You understand the decision-making points in their operating cycles, and of course, the decision makers.

You begin to understand each sector's challenges in the present, and you amass a fair notion of their future challenges. This information has the potential to make you both operationally and strategically relevant to these industries.

At this point, your insight has moved from a functional insight into how to best deliver your current small-niche-band skills, to a strategic insight about what complementary small-niche-band skills you might form. If you are playing football, your field of vision has moved from the tackle in front of you to the broader playing field; you are now more of a quarterback than a defensive blocker. The more you do this, the broader and deeper your insight becomes, and the more your field of vision expands, until you have an eagle's eye view of the playing field, like a coach's vision.

Once you have the coach's vision, you begin to see the permutations and combinations of growth tactics, each collection forming its own strategy, and each strategy imbued with its own pros and cons. You visualize possible growth pathways from the short list of services you provide today to a much longer list of linked services you could provide, and a road map of sequencing how you might grow your service offerings from today's list to tomorrow's list.

You've done all of this from selecting just two, three, or four sectors.

The lists—both today's and tomorrow's—are not static. They change. You should review them frequently, perhaps every few months, with a mind that is completely open to change. Today's list will change as you grow, and it should—of course—primarily change through accretion (adding new services), not through substitution (ditching and replacing old services). It should be emphasized that if you need to remove a service offering (perhaps because it is becoming chronically unprofitable, or the market is shrinking or becoming too commoditized for you), then you should. However, if you are doing this, you should reflect that your initial choice to adopt that service offering may have been flawed, and learn from that mistake.

If you are careful about which services you add to your firm, and in which sequence you accrue them, you create a consistent growth pathway. The question of when to grow will be addressed in the next chapter. But, if you have this growth pathway, and you recast it frequently to guide the implementation of your growth strategy, you now have a blueprint for growth. It is a flexible and adaptable blueprint, which makes it an excellent entrepreneurial tool.

Markets display a considerable amount of cyclic behavior. And while it is certainly unwise to rely solely on cyclic patterns to make your growth decisions, you would be equally unwise to ignore the fact that cycles can, and do, occur. Cycles are often manifest as corrections in supply, demand, and disruption characteristics within your economy of interest. So if there is more supply than demand, prices go down, supply excess is progressively removed from the market and we drift toward equilibrium. We may overshoot equilibrium, giving us an excess of demand over supply, lifting prices and attracting new supply entrants to the market. And so it goes, the elasticity creates the cycles we observe.

The consulting world is a service industry dealing in knowledge and problem solving, and it displays those elastic characteristics as much as another industry. It has, like other industries, interdependencies on other sectors—in this case the client sectors that it services. Those client sectors are, in turn, subject to market elasticity. Picking the sectors and services that are part of an upward phase of their cycles (and preferably in the early upward phases, so that you have a longer run of success) is part of the art of growing.

If the time between the inception of your enterprise and the all-important exit is a few years, then picking upswing sector winners and upswing service winners is a good strategy. Of course, the global financial crisis (the GFC) of 2008 was a rule breaker as it somewhat indiscriminately tore through a wide variety of sectors in a stunning domino effect. It wasn't part of a cyclic event, at least not in the way we had thought of cycles. It was a whole new mechanism of failure. Conventional wisdom would not have prepared us for the GFC.

Post-GFC, while there are regional tremors and warnings of future disruptions, cyclic economic processes seem to continue. With "sustainable" commodities, this makes sense. Supply and demand is a tango, with supply swinging over demand, then the pendulum reversing to correct, and overcorrection a constant beat of the tune.

Those are the mechanics of picking what you do. The science behind your choices of sectors and services helps you to identify and sequence your growth path. Equally important, if not more so, is that your choices energize you. Remember, you are growing a company. Your employees feed off your energy. So choose carefully from that list the things you, as a professional, genuinely want to do. Choose some things that will keep you, the owner, enthusiastic and vibrant.

Of course, it is highly unlikely that the sector that is on an upward trend, the service that's emerging or sustainable and has more demand than supply, *and* the thing that floats your boat personally is also coincidentally the most profitable thing to do. That would be a minor miracle. And so you have tradeoffs to consider and choices to make, none of which will necessarily result in your company being a stunningly profitable funhouse. But that is part of the intrigue of the journey, creating your unique balance that is both profitable and engaging.

Naturally, you'll never know if the choices you did not make could have made you more successful. You'll only know if the choices you make *were* successful in their own right, and whether they kept you energized. You may make choices that are less profitable in the short term, but you may believe they propagate your growth better.

March to your own tune, not everyone else's. In a competitive world, the most attractive propositions will be the sectors and—particularly—the services that are the most profitable. The most attractive propositions, by their definition, attract the most competitors. In that scenario—in most cases at least—supply soon exceeds demand, fueled by a "gold rush" dynamic. Those services have a long-run deterioration in profitability if there is an element of price competitiveness in the market. In other words, if there are too many of you offering the same service, prices go down, margins get squeezed and everyone loses something. In very few cases, where clients buy high-end quality with a lesser regard for price, it is possible to stay above the rabble. But your strategy, to borrow from a basketball metaphor, should be based on high-percentage two-pointer shots, not low-percentage three-pointers.

There is a subtlety here. I am not suggesting that you ignore obvious high-profit services. Quite the opposite in fact. There is nothing wrong, and many things right, with being an active part of "gold rush" propositions. Just don't pivot your growth strategy on them, and don't assume gold rush scenarios last for very long. Use them to provide rapid cash flow to allow you to grow the things that have a longer, steadier life and are more sustainable in the business environment.

The most successful entrepreneur consultants always deliberately choose some services that they, as an individual, have a passion for. It doesn't work as well if you don't. Particularly in problem-solving consultancies, creativity comes from passion. Success stories are littered with examples of entrepreneurs who knew their choices might be less profitable in the short term, but more engaging, sustainable and stable in the long term. They focus on turning these services into signature offerings by investing senior time in developing a high level of consistent quality in the way they provided the services. These "signature services" are almost never the cash cows that most consultants chase with feverish excitement, but they are quietly, confidently, and sustainably valuable to the sectors they applied to.

These choices fuel growth if the portfolio of services you create meets two prerequisites. One is that they are bankable services for the sectors you want to work in; even if some are new and emerging, but with significant prospects for a 5 to 10-year outlook. The other prerequisite is that the choices fuel your own individual enthusiasm, which in turn infects your staff. The first gives you a stable proposition. The second is integral to what a very successful entrepreneur referred to as a "kick-ass culture of growth." Never underestimate the power of both. One gives you the cash flow and security to grow confidently, and the other creates internal excitement and energy, within you and your staff, to chase sustainable growth.

THREE TIPS

Tip 1: Think in cells. A larger enterprise is made up of deliberately chosen, complementary cells—and thinking in cells breaks down a complex proposition into a simpler one for you to strategize around.

Tip 2: Structuring your organization around sectors and services allows you to be more specific about your presence in the market, and it allows you to keep a perspective on where you are and where you want to be in that market.

Tip 3: A strategy formed around "cells" allows you to build nimbleness and resilience in your organization, and—like Lego blocks—it makes the building of your enterprise more flexible and resilient. Think about how your cells fit together, and how they can be independent of each other in how they respond to market upturns and downturns.

5

Grow with Purpose

Do, or do not. There is no try.

Yoda

MECHANICS OF GROWTH

Growing: Every living thing does it without trying. For most living organisms it just happens. We don't think about it. There is no strategy involved in growing. There is a chemical and biological sequence that occurs, and your son or daughter or nephew or niece grows another inch in height.

Nature knows when to grow. Businesses are not necessarily blessed with that insight.

Growth opportunities abound in consulting. In the previous chapter, we looked at the directions in which your company could grow, and we established that the bigger your company becomes, the more options you have for growth. Then, if the markets in those sectors or services can support growth, you have real opportunities.

But opportunities for growth come with risk. Your ability to manage that risk will determine whether you grow successfully or not. There are three focal risks to watch as you develop and execute a growth strategy.

Cash flow is one of the most significant risks in growing. Growth depletes reserves while you are nurturing it. If your reserves deplete, your ability to manage cash flow diminishes. If your ability to manage cash flow falls too far, you begin to trade without liquidity. You are unable to pay your bills as and when they become due (the most significant bill in consulting being your payroll), and your business crashes. Every growth step you take should be buffered by sufficient liquidity (cash, or items that can be converted to cash quickly) to cover both the effort of growing and the possible things that might go wrong. Consulting businesses often fail because growth is attempted while the market softens. Reserves are poured into growth, and at the same time client demand drops off, exposing a large gap in cash flow.

There is such a thing as an unhealthy pace of growth. It is difficult to recognize, in the euphoria that comes with growth, but it exists. Growth that consistently depletes your reserves, resulting in declining cash flows, is unhealthy. Even if the payoff is substantial, the pace of growth can be too fast, and your cash flow can fail before your payoff is achieved. Then, no matter how inspired your strategy was, your business loses.

The second growth risk is the risk of disjointing your brand. Any growth strategy you put in place should have accruing value to the business, building on its core business and amplifying or extending its existing strengths. An extreme example of disjointed growth is, for example, if you add to your accounting firm a growth cell that consults in architecture; or if you add to your law firm a growth cell that consults in project management. The existing business and the growth cell may both be valuable in their own right. However, if you continue to add disjointed cells, you risk losing your company's niche focus, and consequently your company's brand value may be diluted and lost.

To manage this risk well, keep going back to your Exit Strategy. What is it that you want the firm—the one that you will eventually sell—to be recognized for? What will make it attractive to a buyer or an investor? Which services, in which sectors? What is your elevator speech to a prospective buyer?

The third risk of growing is leaving your people behind. Remember that key part of your Exit Strategy … your management team? The team that makes you all but redundant. The team that you need to grow to run a successful business, under your general direction. As you grow your cells and add new cells, you want people to take ownership for growth and grow with you. You want your managers of small teams to grow to be managers of bigger teams, or of offices, or of a cluster of offices.

This risk manifests itself in quite an innocuous way. Some consulting firms grow their cells using imported talent. They may start a new cell, and hire a new person to lead that cell. Or they may grow a cell, and poach someone from another firm to lead that cell. And while this is sometimes—at face value—the most practical and effective way of achieving growth, it fails to bring your existing people with you. Bringing in leaders from outside is often a necessary and pragmatic step, but think carefully about nurturing your own talent, creating internal ownership of growth, and building the Exit Strategy management team from the people you have. It is surprising how passionately your first few employees, allowed growth through your firm, fill the space that you create as you prepare for your exit.

From the last chapter, you should have a sequence of cell development mapped out. Earlier, we have identified cash flow, brand cohesion, and bringing your people along as three key mitigants to the risks of growing. But how do you know *when* to grow?

Let's have a look at a typical business planning cycle in a consulting firm. Some growth targets are set—perhaps 10% or 20% growth in revenues, or perhaps profit—and opportunities are sought to deliver this growth. Why 10% or 20%? There may be no reason, other than that these numbers sound reasonable (and they are round numbers, which is always a handy thing to communicate). So we typically set a target and try to grow to meet the target.

As management processes go, this is pretty uninspired, but at least it's generally practical. You set stretch targets and achieve some or all of that stretch. The goal creates the energy to grow, opportunities are hunted down, some work and some don't, and on a good year you may achieve 60% or 70% of your target. You incentivize your office managers to grow, and pay out bonuses when growth is achieved. It's a traditional and bankable way to grow.

Any business growth should achieve both increase in revenue and increase in profits, ideally commensurate with each other. If your business revenues grow by 20% and your profits grow by 20%, this is a good outcome. If business revenues grow by only 10% but profits grow by 20%, this is also a good outcome. If the business revenues grow 20% but the profits only grow 10%, this is a fair outcome but it raises questions about the efficiency of growth.

Clearly though, you do not want business revenues to go up and profits to go down; nor do you want business revenues and profits to go down. Neither of these two really qualifies as growth.

And what of sustainable growth? How do you grow continuously, aggregating as you go? Is sustainable growth simply a series of successful set-and-achieve target years, a Groundhog Day of meeting key performance indicators?

My observations over a quarter century showed there were two common factors that consulting firms displayed when they set and pursued growth targets. Common Factor 1 was that most consulting professionals had little or no training in growing successful businesses. They were lawyers, accountants, doctors, engineers, scientists, architects, advertising executives, psychologists, or any number of professional practitioners, but—in most cases—they were not trained in growing businesses. Some had an uncanny knack for growing, others were hit-and-miss, and others failed spectacularly. But overall, they—as a professional species—had no business being asked to grow a consulting practice.

Common Factor 2 was that all of these professionals fell into one of two simple categories. One category was what I called the born-again accountant; a professional who would become mesmerized by a profit and loss account, and whose growth strategies largely hinged upon leveraging the numbers in the two columns of this account. The other category was what I called the maverick, who disregarded conventional wisdom and just grew by instinct.

No matter how many successful consultants I asked, no one had a clear answer for why they were successful at growing. When pressed, many of these successful consultants would paint a picture of a business acumen that contained some rigorous processes and some mystical powers of foresight.

So when I started my first consulting firm, I was looking for a decision-making process that—as closely as possible—automated growth. Or, more precisely, told you when to grow. I had been an executive for a large company for a few years by that stage, and I realized that growth strategies were part art, part science.

While I appreciated and respected that some mystical powers could be useful, and I often marveled at those managers who displayed those powers, I personally wanted as little as possible of the dark arts in my methodology. It allowed for too many interpretations of signals for growth. At its worst, it allowed "forced growth" to occur, resulting in growth spurts that were reversed within months, leading to wasted resources in achieving the growth, and evaporated profits in dealing with the pain of downsizing. At its most mediocre, it led to contract labor practices, increasing the unit cost of labor while harnessing temporary growth, creating an illusion of growth and prosperity.

Managers grow their consulting units or offices for many reasons. Some are purely egotistical, empire-building reasons. Others, driven by a key performance indicator from their own manager, or a head office mandate, achieve short-term growth (and hence their short-term bonus) in 1 year.

If growth foundations are poor, the growth can be reversed the next year and no short-term bonus gained. But a bonus in 1 year followed by no bonus the next year is better than no bonus at all over 2 years, so there is no disincentive for this unsustainable practice.

My research showed that there were some examples of sustained growth, but I was appalled that for every such example I could point to several other abject failures. In fact, unsustainable or periodic growth-and-shrink patterns were more prominent in the consulting landscape than not.

But before we look at the mechanics of sustainable growth, let us understand the relationship between growth and profit.

PROFIT VERSUS GROWTH

To manage any enterprise, understanding the finances is crucial. From capital spending to cash flow, managing monetary matters ranks as one of the top skills required by managers and leaders. Unfortunately, as we noted before in this chapter, not all of us are trained in finance. If you have a valuable consulting skill, and it's not based on capital spending and cash flow, where does that leave you when you are trying to grow an office or to grow a service in a consulting firm? It leaves you poorly prepared.

If you are ever in the position where you can watch, for a few years, managers in large consulting companies deal with this skills mismatch, it is a revealing experience. You will realize that a layman's view of a profit and loss statement is a dangerously limiting thing. Everyone understands that profit is revenue minus expenditure. There is nothing magical in that equation. If it costs me $1.50 to make a hot dog and I sell it for $2.50, my profit is $1.

In consulting, because you are creating value with human resources and supporting expenditure, expenditure is largely within your control. To make your hot dog on the other hand, you rely on market costs of the bread roll, the sausage, the mustard, and the ketchup. Although you can make choices about where and how you buy these things, you are in a supply chain and there is only so much you can do about the things that happen before we get to your link of the chain. You certainly can't influence the price of sausages or the cost of the bottle of mustard. So if you are asked to increase your profit by 20 cents, there is only so much give in the expenditure line. If your costs remain at $1.50 and you want to increase your profit by 20 cents, you will charge $2.70 instead of $2.50. And if your costs increase to $1.70, you will charge $2.90.

Contrast this with consulting. It is not within a classic supply chain. Most of your value resides in people's heads. You have a set of overheads that you support to keep people happy, creative, and productive in extracting the value from their brains. Office space, desks, computers, air conditioning, biscuits, coffee, marketing budgets, decor, and many others are part of the set of overheads you provide.

If I ask a consulting manager to increase profits by 5% (with a bonus incentive, of course), the *easiest* thing to do is to reduce expenditure because my supply chain is very short. Of course, the manager will take a shot at increasing revenue (I hope). But it's uncertain whether he or she will attain revenue goals because the market is competitive. To be more confident of achieving profit margins, it's easier to tackle the known quantities. Look at the expenditure list, and seek ways of reducing it. Obvious questions arise. Why do we need so much office space? Why are the bonuses for junior people so generous? Business class and first class flights … why? And why on earth do we need chocolate biscuits? Haven't you heard that sugar is the new axis of evil?

In most cases, it's perfectly possible to Scrooge your way into a higher profit margin. This is not automatically a bad thing, because frivolous expenditure will harm any enterprise, and a little bit of Scrooge in manageable doses is healthy. But if it becomes a runaway method of management, it risks achieving the reverse of what you would hope for. It risks lower productivity, lower creativity, greater turnover, and—let's face it—it risks creating a place that is not fun to work in.

Consulting managers are generally not blessed with creative business and financial management skills. Lawyers, engineers, graphic designers, advertising consultants, and even economists are not taught that expenditure reduction is a limited strategy. You can only do so much before the floor of your expenditures hits the basement. The revenue roof, on the other hand, can keep extending to the sky. These are not insights they teach at engineering school or law school, obvious as they are.

As a younger consultant, I had excellent consulting mentors, some of whom had IQs of Einsteinian proportions. But this one-dimensional ability to navigate a profit and loss statement was often their Achilles' heel. Incredibly talented consulting managers could simply not create sustainable growth. They could talk the hind leg off a donkey, sell ice to

Eskimos, and find solutions to problems whose complexity you would not have believed existed. But they could not do what their 10-year-old child did every day—grow continuously, relentlessly.

Instead, most growth was achieved by planning, taking a deep breath and injecting growth funds. This could be done in two ways.

You could, for example, buy a successful business and assimilate it into your arsenal. This is a bit like growing by grafting a third arm onto your armpit. You *do* grow. Your weight increases by a few percent. You get more done because, as we all know, many hands make light work. Your revenue increases and if you assimilate well, your profitability increases.

You could find some money to invest in a new sector or new service, nurture it and grow it. This is quite sensible provided you can find some money. Sometimes, this is a big *if*. When it's just you and perhaps a few people in your consulting firm, bankrolling investments can be a challenge.

So, funding growth with specific injections of cash is both possible and normal. You make a decision to grow in a certain way, you do your business planning, you find the money, you inject it, and you work to get your return on investment.

But what if you want to grow more continuously and organically, and with operating cash flow only? What if you want to make growth a natural part of your business, rather than an occasional and excruciatingly considered momentous decision?

> When I developed my first consulting firm, it required just a modest amount of cash. The house was refinanced to allow for this.
>
> I had a deep aversion toward debt. Now, a pathological dislike of debt is not financially astute; but there you go, that's what I had in my psychological makeup. As I pointed out before, consultants are typically not bred with any kind of keen financial insights.
>
> From that initial investment, the company grew dramatically without having to inject any more growth funds into it. At some points, cash flow was a delicate balancing act, but the growth, across four continents, was steady, continuous and one of the fastest in the market.
>
> Some years later, after this first consulting company was sold, I calculated the return on investment on that modest mortgage extension at about 220% per year, compounding. This was, admittedly, off a small investment, which isn't going to affect world economics, although it was clearly a very efficient way to increase wealth. The return on investment occurred without incurring debt in the company, or incurring further personal debt. In other words, there was no further debt leverage.

I didn't realize how remarkable the average compounding rate of return on the investment was, until I had sold the firm and was figuring out what to do next. I was discussing, with a number of potential investors, a copper mining prospect that we were considering, for which I was invited to sit on the board. One of the investors was a 75-year-old high net worth individual, a former football star from the 1960s who had turned entrepreneur and had created and sold successful businesses for most of his life. I was awed by his track record of brilliant investments, and sheepishly kept any details of my one modest success to myself. We were discussing the return on investment of the potential copper mine over several years, and considering floating the entity on the stock exchange. Naturally, this would result in a very healthy return on investment for all of us, but somewhat short of the 220% per year I had experienced before. We were poring over financial projections and discussing options over lunch. I mused out loud that we should work through the concept more and see if we could hit an average rate of return of 150% or 200% per year.

The high net worth individual looked at me, startled.

"We'd need to find high grade gold in there as well, if we're to consider anything like that kind of return," he replied gruffly. The other directors looked at me bemused, and the looks on their faces indicated that my financial credibility had dropped quite a few percentage points in their estimation.

I suddenly doubted if I had gotten my calculation right for my own first consulting investment, years before. When I went home that weekend, I dug out the financial records from that consulting enterprise and recalculated the return on investment. It didn't change; I hadn't made a mistake. There must have been some high grade gold in our approach back then.

GROWING WITHOUT GROWING PAINS

There are three ingredients I always try to bake into a consulting business, and I advise others of the same. I believe that if you achieve all three, it's almost impossible to avoid success. The first is a more "automated" decision-making process for growth, particularly answering the "when to grow" question. The second is that managers apply a profit focus that does not default to the control of expenditure as their main game. The third is self-funded growth; in other words, if you can manage it, don't borrow to create growth. I'm aware the last is not conventional wisdom; it's a personal preference. However, after the global financial crisis, it probably does qualify as some kind of wisdom.

When I started my first entrepreneurial venture, I had a theoretical answer to the "how to" question that gave me all three desirable outcomes, but I had never put it into practice. While doing my MBA, many years before, I had written my thesis on the development of a global consulting business. The thesis looked at international growth and business roll-out models in Asia, and wasn't overly technical. But while thinking through the practicalities of developing businesses, I developed a theoretical model for growth that addressed the three ingredients I wanted to apply to consulting businesses. The theoretical model was based on financial ratios, which are used by most directors and financial analysts in assessing the health of a company through, primarily, its balance sheet and profit and loss statements. Financial ratios are simply one metric divided by another, and a combination of ratios can be used to "see" the patterns that lie within the company's financial documents.

When I started my first consulting firm, I dusted this model off, and it formed the basis of the red-wine/Spider-Man lecture in Chapter 2 that I delivered to my two colleagues.

The theory works this way. Obviously, the relationship that profit equals revenue minus expenditure is simple, and everyone gets it. But it's too simple, and it would be seductively easy for people to focus overly on expenditure as a "cheap" way to maximize profit. So the theory begins by breaking every rule regarding keeping it simple, and complicates the humble profit equation.

Let's make a set of very straightforward assumptions that apply well to consulting. The first is that you are paying people to use their brains, therefore your prime asset is people and their prime cost is their salaries. You use their salaries to earn fees, so your key lever is the ratio of fees to salaries. The higher the ratio of fees to salaries, the better the leverage. If fees are f and salaries are s, the following ratio is very important to you,

$$\frac{f}{s}$$

The other straightforward assumption is that you need to control costs, but that the costs are simply supporting your people. Your total costs, tc, are the sum of your salary costs, s, and the supporting costs—call them overheads—c. In other words,

$$tc = s + c$$

Your lever on costs can be expressed as

$$\frac{s}{tc}$$

You don't want this to get too small; in other words don't allow your overhead costs to dominate and therefore make the denominator too large. The cost lever can only be as high as 1.0, which is when you have no supporting costs and you put Scrooge to shame.

These two ratios, *f/s* and *s/tc*, became my two driving performance indicators. But what are good ratios, as opposed to average or poor ratios? How do they relate to profits and profitability? For the answer, let's rewrite the profit and loss account in terms of these ratios.

The humble profit equation is

$$\text{Profit} = \text{Revenue} - \text{Expenditure}$$

which in our language is fees less total costs, or

$$\text{Profit} = f - tc$$

Profitability, which is your percentage profit, is your profit divided by your net revenue (or the proportion of your revenue—your fees—that settles comfortably in the bank).

$$\frac{Profit}{f} = 1 - \frac{tc}{f}$$

which is the same as saying

$$Profitability = 1 - \frac{tc}{f}$$

which, by some simple algebra, is identical to

$$Profitability = 1 - \frac{1}{\left(\dfrac{f}{s}\right)\left(\dfrac{s}{tc}\right)}$$

For those readers unfamiliar with, afraid of, or simply irritated by algebra, I apologize for this departure into college mathematics. However, I urge you to try and understand it, because it will unlock insights into the financial potential in your consulting company and allow you to direct your managers toward growth in a way that makes the best use of their strengths—their consulting abilities—without enticing them to develop growth-inhibiting behaviors from their studious and mostly untrained analysis of their profit and loss statements.

The two ratios give you two simple levers with which to guide your managers in growth. They are not all the knowledge that is required to grow, as someone (you) needs to analyze your profit and loss statements, your balance sheet and your cash flow. But you can use these two levers to empower your managers to create organic growth.

The final equation relates the two ratios to profitability. We now need to understand what combinations of the two ratios give you the kind of profitability you want, and what is practical. Figure 5.1 shows how one lever (plotted on the horizontal axis) relates to the other, and translates into profitability. It shows zones that are generally impractical, a zone that is technically profitable but potentially mediocre, and a zone that represents high profits and balanced success.

The figure contains a wealth of information, and it is worth examining closely. It shows the translation to profitability and identifies the zone of success. The horizontal axis is the fees-to-salary ratio, plotted from 1.0 to 3.0. The vertical axis is profitability, plotted from minus 80% (a disaster) to plus 80% (which is improbably high).

The series of curves plots the profitability against fees-to-salary ratios, for a range of salary-to-total cost ratios. The salary-to-total cost ratios plotted vary from 0.5 (extremely high overheads) to 1.0 (impossibly tight, no overheads, and a cost-management effort Scrooge would be proud of).

Fees-to-salary and salary-to-total-cost ratios are the two guiding financial key performance indicators for consulting cells and offices. The fees-to-salary ratio is the driving force. If we are riding a bicycle, they are the pedals. The salary-to-total cost ratio is much easier to manage and only needs fine adjustments most of the time, like the handlebars of a bicycle.

From the graph, it is then a matter of picking your target. Let's say your salary-to-total cost ratio sits at around 0.7. At a fees-to-salary ratio of 2.2, profitability is around 35%. This is not hard to do if your managers' operating behaviors are right. And most business owners salivate over profits like that.

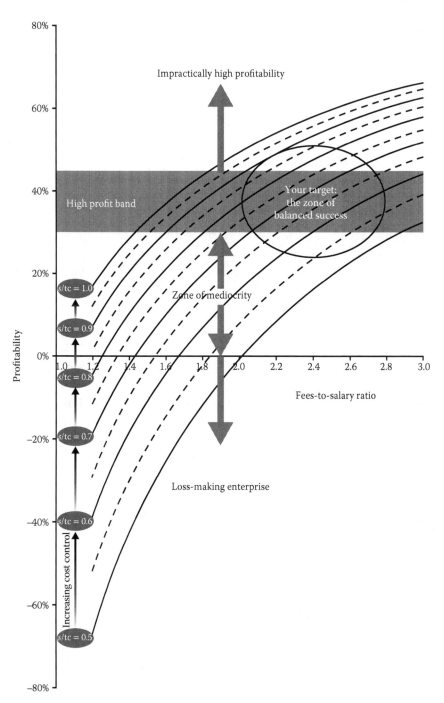

FIGURE 5.1
Fees-to-salary growth and profit diagram.

The reality is that all businesses meander around this graph. Good strategy, good marketing, and great execution of projects will keep you in the grey zone, but it is normal to fall into the more mediocre zones from time to time. This graph is not meant to be a key performance indicator, although it does give you that information; it is meant to tell you *when* to grow.

Most small companies make 10% to 15% profit. Profits of 20% and 25% are generally very good. Some large construction firms refuse to bid for projects under $400 million, and their profits are 12% to 14% on a good year. Legal and accounting firms are a lot more lucrative, and a profitability in the low 20s is not uncommon. A consulting firm I worked in had once made 17% in a year, and the celebrations had been orgasmic.

You can choose to grow at any fees-to-salary threshold that your analysis shows to be correct for you. By the time you have four or five staff, you will know what your growth threshold is. My own philosophy is to set it high, like revving the engine of a stick shift before moving up a gear. The fees-to-salary threshold was well above 2.0, which meant that growth was triggered when we had sustained profitability at 30% or more.

By year three of my first consulting effort, we had grown very strongly, running two national offices and two international offices. Our profitability was high and we were a significant threat to our competitors; both for their clients and for their staff.

I recall our financial manager walking into my office one afternoon, a quizzical expression on her face and two magazines in her hand. One was *Forbes* magazine, and the other was a national business magazine liftout that was published one day in each month in a national newspaper.

"We should be in this list," she said earnestly, but still with that quizzical expression on her face. I asked what list she was thinking of. She opened the *Forbes* magazine, which had an article on the most profitable start-up businesses of the last few years, and the business magazine, which had the country's "Hot 100" growth businesses, and profiles of their owners.

She was right. *Forbes* listed Tier One companies—the most profitable companies—at an average profitability of 16.5%. The top five or six of the Hot 100 had year-on-year growth rates (growth in revenues) of 50% or more over 3 year averages. Our profitability was about twice the average of that of *Forbes'* Tier One firms, and we were easily in the revenue growth rate bracket of the top five or six in the country.

She was quizzical because it didn't seem right. And it's true; it felt surreal. But the numbers didn't lie. I pointed out that we did, to be fair, distribute a lot of that profit, and we used much of the profit to start up new businesses and grow. So gross profit wasn't the best measure, and perhaps we weren't really comparing apples with apples in this case. Still, it was a flattering realization that our performance put us in the company of some enviably successful businesses.

GETTING YOUR MANAGERS TO GROW

Translating this model to growth is reasonably straightforward. If you have a mandate to grow, every manager of every cell should be focused on that mandate. A simple automatic rule might be that if a cell meets a fees-to-salary ratio of 2.3 or above for 3 months in a row, it should grow. The actual number (typically in the range 2.0–2.6, but entirely up to you) is calculated based on your Exit Strategy. If you are less aggressive in growth and more profit focused, you might choose a fees-to-salary ratio of 2.5 or more. Track fees-to-salary ratios weekly, and if a cell's prognosis for the second or third month in a row is looking good, you might initiate a growth conversation with the manager of that cell, or the general manager of the cluster of cells in that office.

Any consulting business can define its own metrics using fees-to-salary and salary-to-total cost. The trick is not so much to set the goals; it is to manage the process of meeting or exceeding them.

Of course, not every growth conversation results in an automatic decision to grow. It is important to consider whether growth is sustainable, and not just growth for the sake of growth. Be judicious about choices to grow. What the process does is to focus each of your managers on profitability through fees and the growth model, rather than the cost control model of low growth profitability. It means that you can continually—and by continually I do mean every month and every quarter—address one or more growth prospects.

When you grow multiple offices, the balance of the fees-to-salary model becomes more of an art form. Think of playing an instrument, and then think of conducting a small orchestra. The pace of growth is different for each office—in other words each instrument has a different part to play—but the overriding model applies for the whole organization. So your whole orchestra may be geared, for example, to a fees-to-salary ratio of say 2.2, but individual offices may run at 2.5, or 2.1, or 2.0.

A word of caution—this orchestration needs a lot of concentration if you want to manage it well. Your role as the conductor is critical. In one company that used this model, as we grew internationally, the pace of growth became frenetic, and complicated by foreign exchange considerations, tax implications, and sovereign risk issues. Think of those instruments, playing not in a controlled amphitheater, but on a gusty beach where sound travels and dissipates. In those circumstances, your orchestration is critical.

The cell model, the fees-to-salary model of profitability and the growth mandate at fees-to-salaries of [insert your number here!] means that you can have multiple drivers of growth and profit throughout the business. Managers and general managers don't need to look at profit and loss accounts at any other time than the end of a financial year. At that point, their scrutiny of the profit-and-loss accounts is a review of the year just gone, an assessment of the trends and the underlying reasons for them, and—using those reflections—planning for the year or two ahead. Their scrutiny of the profit and loss account is not operationally essential to running the business if they manage these two ratios. It adds contextual value to improving, year on year, the way they manage their business.

Their key performance indicators are clear and simple, and focused on profitability and growth. Under those conditions, running a business is noticeably simplified, and it makes time in their schedule as managers to focus on the people aspects of your business (both client service and employee engagement), where the real value lies.

THREE TIPS

Tip 1: The profit and loss account, that stalwart of accountants everywhere, is useful and necessary for your tax requirements, if nothing else. It may not be the best dashboard for your managers. Remember that the people you hire—the talented consultants—are often not natural-born (or adequately trained) business managers or business growth specialists. Give them simple management and growth models to work with, or be prepared to invest depressingly heavily in their business management skills!

Tip 2: High profit, high growth is perfectly feasible if you think in cells, growth thresholds, and topline revenues. Don't settle for low profit, high growth; or high profit, low growth. That's what everyone else does, and it merely breeds an average enterprise.

Tip 3: Keep your discipline. You might incentivize your entire organization, to grow, but pick where you grow and when. Grow when you are ready to grow, and grow in cells so that you minimize risk.

6

Debt-Free Growth

Money often costs too much.

Ralph Waldo Emerson

GROWTH FUNDS AND GROWTH RATES

Growing any business involves spending money. If you have a growing grocery store, you have to spend more money on stock, or on an extension to your shop, and perhaps new staff. You need more infrastructure and more systems to run a bigger business. Your accounts are more complicated, so your accountants' bills increase. In growing any business, you must brace yourself for increasing expenditure. Of course, the expectation is that you will also increase income, and that the sustainable increase in income will be greater than the expenditure that you incur.

Spending for business growth is an investment, and many business owners rationalize that borrowing to invest (provided you can pay it back in a reasonable timeframe) is OK. Actually, it is OK. But what is even better is to grow as much as you can without borrowing funds.

The way to do this, of course, is to put aside excess income until you have enough funds to pay for your growth out of your working capital or your operational cash flow.

Before pursuing this subject, it should be pointed out that it is not at all unwise to borrow money to grow. There is a reason that banks have been around for a long time. Borrowing money to grow works; it has been a successful practice for hundreds of years, and it is beneficial for both lender and borrower. Sometimes it is unavoidable. For example, if you want to own your own home, you are likely to start off by going into debt. But it can be mind-numbing, future-limiting debt. Yet it is often a necessary evil. And while many people might manage to coexist with it, surely you, me, and every other entrepreneur are at our happiest without debt.

In growing a consulting business, as you would have gathered from the fees-to-salary ratios and the salary-to-total cost ratios, the key to debt-free growth is balancing labor cost and corresponding consulting income throughout your growth increments. Labor cost is your highest expenditure, and your labor pool defines your growth and size. Consulting fees are, at their core, hourly rates. So, the balance you seek, at each step of growth, is ensuring that every new person you hire is more than covered by a commensurate increase in consulting fees. Meanwhile, the investment in systems and processes for your growing firm, your higher accounting fees, compliance requirements and ancillary staff such as human resources might be initially funded by the cash reserves you have already built, and sustained funding comes from the income from the fees that are earned.

In the last chapter, we concluded that balancing profitability and growth is an art. You have to pay close attention to the present and the near future, predict the things that may change in each, and act accordingly. Being profitable and growing, without falling into debt, is a challenging proposition. But it can be done.

Of course, we are unanimous in our agreement that it is better to grow without debt than it is to grow using borrowed funds. But, to break it down, there are four very good reasons for growing a successful business without borrowing. First, you are focusing on growing a noncapital intensive business; such businesses are not particularly hungry for cash outside of labor costs and so the balance between labor cost-based growth funds and labor-based income is relatively easy to predict. Second, owing anyone money—the burden of debt—is something most people find stressful, and genuinely dislike. Third, the more you owe, the less control you have of your own destiny (although admittedly you can negotiate around this one in lending agreements so that you don't inadvertently lose your independence to your lender). Finally—quite simply—because you can.

Now, there is a limit to how much and how fast you can grow without borrowing. It is not particularly feasible to shepherd significant growth perpetually without borrowing to provide cash injections into your business. So if you are determined to grow without borrowing, remember that in all likelihood there is only so much growth you will be able to achieve without borrowing. There will come a time when your rate of growth can no longer increase substantially without injected growth funds. If you carefully plot the path to your Exit Strategy by analyzing growth and cash flow, you will understand what that horizon looks like for you.

Doing your arithmetic comprehensively before the start of your enterprise journey is important. Obviously, unless you're channeling a particularly accurate soothsayer, your predictions will, more likely than not, be incorrect. What is more important than accuracy is that you understand your assumptions and what they mean to your business growth and its financing—and that you are ready to reforecast your plan if one or more of your assumptions proves to be wrong. It is a little-acknowledged but powerful part of the discipline of entrepreneurs. Plan it in excruciating detail, then expect it all to change. Getting it right is not as important as understanding the mechanics of how you can grow.

GROWING IN FEES-TO-SALARY INCREMENTS

In Chapter 5, we introduced the concept of the signal to grow, based on a target fees-to-salary ratio and a short, sustained period of cell and enterprise performance at a fees-to-salary target. The signal to grow is only one aspect of what you need to look at. The other is, of course, whether you have enough reserve cash for the extra salary cost and the total cost of growing.

Figure 5.1 in Chapter 5 demonstrated the strong profitability of high target fees-to-salary ratios and well-controlled salary-to-total cost ratios. Every month that you operate at those targets nets extra cash, which accumulates to provide you with growth funds out of working capital. However, expect that after each growth step, your fees-to-salary ratio takes a small tumble and you need to reestablish high-performance ratios for a while before you accumulate the cash for the next growth step.

Let us look at a 5-year run of a consulting office that follows a fees-to-salary growth model. In this model, the consulting firm grows by one person when it achieves a fees-to-salary ratio of 2.3 for 2 months in a row. The number of consultants grows steadily (Figure 6.1).

Your fees-to-salary ratio looks a little bit like this sawtooth curve (Figure 6.2), for each new person you hire at regular intervals.

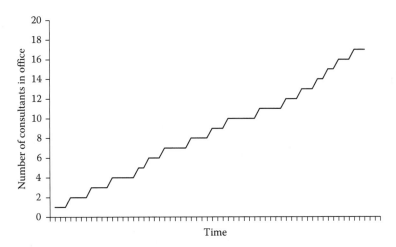

FIGURE 6.1
Paced growth in number of consultants.

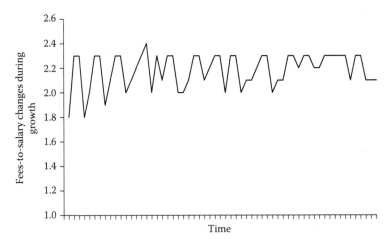

FIGURE 6.2
Fees-to-salary fluctuations during growth steps.

As your business grows, the fees-to-salary ratio dip experienced by each new hire gets progressively smaller. Quite predictably, it is less impactful to hire a person when you are already 50 or 100 strong, than it was when you were only 10 people strong. The lower impact allows you to fund growth more frequently. This can be done by scheduling new hires in the high-performing cells of your consulting business so that the smaller incremental growth occurs more frequently as you get bigger, accelerating your growth to better than the diminishing return off the baseline.

The continual investment in growth means that short-term profitability is sacrificed to create a sustained increase in profits over time, as shown in Figure 6.3. Note the periodic reductions in profits, which are largely the result of new staff costs and the initially low utilization rates of these staff members.

Despite the ongoing increase in profits, the profit growth rates dwindle, for equivalent cash input, as you grow. When you grow from one fee-earning consultant to two fee-earning consultants, you achieve—nominally—100% profit growth. You do this with one extra salary cost. When you grow from two fee-earning consultants to three fee-earning consultants, you achieve—nominally—only 50% profit growth for the same quantum of extra salary cost. By the time, you have 100 fee-earning consultants, you only achieve a 1% growth for that same extra salary cost. This is a diminishing return off your baseline, so your growth rate plateaus out. Figure 6.4 shows this effect over a 5-year period. Note the sawtooth shape of the profit growth percentages, and the decay in growth rates over time. So, while it is possible to increase the rate of growth of profits continually over a period of time, the growth rate decreases per unit of invested cost the bigger your firm or office becomes.

Somewhere along your dwindling growth rate, you will decide that you have optimized your growth and it is time to sell. That point, the focus of your Exit Strategy will have balanced two things in your mind—the sale value of your business, and the time it would take to substantially increase that sale value.

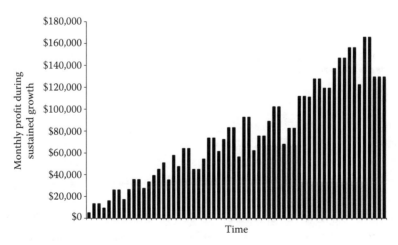

FIGURE 6.3
Monthly profit trend in sustained growth.

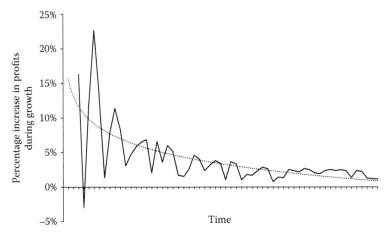

FIGURE 6.4
Percentage increase in profits during sustained growth.

Your method of management then looks something like this.

First, you evaluate every cell's fees-to-salary ratio, as well as the overall business fees-to-salary ratio and the periodic (e.g., monthly) accumulation of working capital.

Second, you consider growth only in the cells that have sustainably well-performing fees-to-salary ratios; or you consider new cells in your business.

Third, you only grow if two other things are evident: (1) your overall business fees-to-salary is high and (2) your working capital accumulated is more than sufficient to cover the extra costs associated with growth. Do not grow if one or the other is not at, or above, your targets.

CASH IS KING

Funding growth without creating an internal financial crisis is a delicate balancing act, and one that requires your constant and absolute attention. While achieving self-funded growth is a deeply satisfying experience, it is very taxing (no pun intended). Avoiding the spectre of debt while running a growing business soon becomes an experience that is not unlike juggling while riding a unicycle up a ramp. It requires quite a bit of coordination.

In the last chapter, I expanded on the growth model, and it is necessary to qualify a few things now in order to clarify how to maintain debt-free growth.

The fees-to-salary model usually delivers multiple growth options. Suppose you have 10 consulting cells running, and 4 are operating at fees-to-salary ratios of 2.3 and above for 3 or more months in a row (your key performance indicator relating to growth, as an example). You do not need (or necessarily want) to grow in all four cells simultaneously. You could pick one or two, at the most. There are a number of factors that should be considered before picking these, including but not limited to the nature of the service, its existing and future demand by clients, the breadth of clients presenting with this demand, the attractiveness of other services you could start (i.e., an 11th cell rather than an investment in one of the existing 10 cells), the availability in the market of consultants, how much it would cost to grow and, of course, how much you can afford. The affordability criterion should be dictated, in true cash-is-king form, by how much banked profit has accumulated during the 3 months prior, by all of the cells in operation. There is no need to spend more than you have in the bank; in fact, that would defeat the objective of debt-free growth.

The fees-to-salary ratio is derived from the revenue earned. Most consultancies utilize billable hours, or chargeability, as the key performance indicator, which correlates broadly to revenues. Whichever way you look at it, you cannot grow without increasing revenues, and the rate of growth is directly related to the rate at which you can grow your revenues. So, if you look over a 12-month or 2-year timeframe, your increase in revenues is an essential performance indicator.

What happens when you grow—and this is especially true in consulting firms whose main expenditure is salaries—is that the cost of employment builds rapidly to frighteningly high levels. Because wages are paid at a set time (for example, monthly), each month has a looming and very large expenditure that has absolutely no flexibility in timing. You simply have to pay your salary costs as well as other costs related to personnel, such as taxes and any compulsory superannuation or retirement-fund obligations, on time.

Clients, however, are not faced with the same extreme sensitivity to timing when they pay your bills. In fact, there is often a despairing level of ambivalence by clients to paying bills on time. Work done in month 1 will, if you are lucky, be paid for in month 2 (or more likely in month 3 or even month 4), and some clients have no difficulty in extending this to month 6 or in some extreme cases, year 2.

This creates a volatility problem for the consulting firm. So whereas the year-on-year revenue growth might show a consistent trend, the month-on-month cash inflows can be very "lumpy"—high in one month and low in another—because of your clients' inconsistencies in how and when they pay you. In fact, this "lumpiness" can increase as your business grows.

The "lumpiness" can expose your business to cash shortages that have the potential to put you out of business despite having a strong year-on-year growth in revenues. And the "lumpiness" is significantly exacerbated if your debtors—the clients that owe you money—are not controlled.

Interestingly, it is quite often found that the big client companies are equally, if not more likely, to pay late than smaller client companies. Sometimes this is due to a simple policy of keeping cash in *their* businesses for as long as possible, and the default position might need some effort to budge. Bigger client companies can sometimes have entrenched payment policies that are not amenably open to discussion, whereas smaller companies might have fewer administrative hurdles to overcome default invoice payment policies. In a smaller client company, you might ring the chief financial officer (CFO) and have a friendly chat. It is less likely you will get to the CFO in a multinational corporation, and you might instead find yourself in a circular conversation with a midlevel administrator that goes nowhere quite slowly.

If anything is going to derail your self-funding growth plans, this revenue timing is a strong candidate. Many entrepreneurial consultants with their own growing firms have (wisely, you would have thought) anticipated this trend, but they uniformly reported that they completely underestimated the size of its effect. As your enterprise grows larger, you fall further and further to the mercy of clients who pay late. Where once your bailout funds might cover you for some late payments, eventually the size of the bailout fund that you need looks like a small country's gross domestic product. You sleep less and less soundly at night. You get frustrated with your clients. The compulsion to go into debt to create your buffer becomes almost too much to ignore. How can you get your clients to support your cash flow, and not create a cash flow crisis for you to constantly battle?

SHEPHERDING YOUR DEBTORS

It's very important to develop some kind of custodianship of the revenue loop that runs between your invoicing and the income derived from clients. The first, and most important, part of the custodianship is your relationship with the client. It must be strong enough and warm enough to address, without recrimination, potentially late payments. This issue should be important enough to you that you take a personal stake in client payment timings, at least in the early stages of your enterprise. In practice, this is a relationship that allows you to ring up a client and request timely payments for work done.

The second part of the custodianship is setting the contract arrangements in a way that supports payments on time. The reason this is done is that very often your client contact, the person who made the decision to hire you, has no special relationship with his or her accounting section. So you might lean on him or her to pay on time, but potentially to no avail because he or she has no real reason to take on a battle with the accounting section just for you. Of course, if he or she can point to a contract clause that mandates the payment in a specified time, then there is no "battle," just a commercial reason to pay on time. Such a clause might—ideally—have a compelling disincentive for late payment practices, such as ceasing work (which is a very confronting clause to include in a contract) or a financial penalty (which is more palatable, but still somewhat a touchy subject).

Many larger firms now have supply chain ethics to consider in their procurement divisions, and these ethics are often reflected in their sustainability charter. Often, considerations include enabling small and medium-sized businesses to prosper. These may fall under local content guidelines (which are guidelines that ensure that smaller, local suppliers get a fair go at winning the client's business and thriving on the source of income) or under broader procurement processes that create equitable opportunities for the broader realm of suppliers. These guidelines and processes will often include timely payments of invoices to ensure that smaller enterprises don't die of cash starvation. The client initiatives often exist on paper—in a sustainability policy or guideline—but it is surprising how many clients' accounting sections seem unaware of them. Do your research on a client's policies, and hold the client accountable for meeting their commitments.

The third part is understanding your client's accounting processes. Many late payments are triggered by invoices that raise some kind of accounting, administrative, or contractual question—some ambiguity, missing information, incorrect cost codings or other data. Your invoice goes from the top of the pile in the "in" tray to the "issues pending" tray that hopefully will receive some attention when the "in" tray is empty. And if your client is a large organization, their "in" tray is a perpetually growing beast. You definitely do not want your invoice to lose its place in that tray. And so, trivial as it sounds, having your accounting section applying a very pedantic and client-focused discipline to sending out invoices can save you a lot of financial pain. While this sounds like an obvious tactic, it is surprising how many small consulting firms insist on using a rigid invoicing template, simply because they think it displays professional discipline. It doesn't. The purpose of an invoice is not to look identical to all other invoices; instead, it should aim to be legally compliant and to facilitate a quick payment.

Understanding how to craft your invoices so that each client finds it easy to pay is, literally, gold. Unfortunately, every client has a different set of requirements to achieve this ease. Being flexible enough to make your invoicing bespoke for your clients, or at least the ones receiving big bills, is an advantage. It sounds like extra work, doesn't it? It is. It sounds inefficient, and I won't argue with you on that point. But, inefficient as it is, it is more *effective* to think this way than to nurture some kind of misguided administrative ego that tells you—with a petulant stamp of its foot—that people should pay on time when they receive a bill. It's your business, and cash flow is the lifeblood of your business. Don't risk clogged arteries.

The discipline of shepherding invoices is one of the most powerful disciplines to get right if you want a self-funding growth firm.

SMOOTHING REVENUES

The reality of a consulting business is that cash flow smoothing is difficult to achieve. A significant part of cash flow smoothing is avoiding pinch points in your cash cycle. The end-of-month wages are a pinch point. The flood of revenue from the invoices sent out last month is also another pinch point. Quite bizarrely, most businesses pay wages and do all their invoices at the end of the month. This means that at the end of each month, you are doing two things simultaneously. You are paying a massive bill, and you are sending out requests for revenue. If you think about it logically, that is a painful way to live.

Staggered billing is a useful way to "smear" your revenue stream so that it is more steady. It doesn't solve the problem of course, but it does ease it, and it's psychologically quite calming to see a steady flow of revenue rather than sudden bursts of cash through the door. Even though the sudden bursts of cash might dizzyingly feel like you've won the lottery, I can promise you that your heart can only take so much lottery-winning. It's simply no fun to be holding your breath waiting for lumps of revenue to come in. Take away the lumpiness, and you will live longer.

A surprising percentage of businesses create challenges for themselves because they assume that invoicing needs to be done at a certain time during the month. Most businesses set aside the last 7 days of each month to get invoices out. In that 7 days, a surge of accounts receivables is created and the business is owed an immense amount of money.

There are two simple but effective ways of smoothing your cash flow, and therefore smoothing your revenue cycle. The first is to split your billings; for example, half your clients are billed in the middle of the month, and half your clients are billed at the end of the month. It is surprising just how much of a difference this can make to your cash flow, especially if combined with good client management and invoice shepherding. To make this practical, your time sheet discipline must be high. Your staff must diligently code their time and expenses to the various projects they are working on, so that there are no outstanding time sheets or expenses at the end of each week. If it sounds like a boring piece of advice, that's because it is—but it makes a difference to how efficiently you roll out split billing cycles. Some firms run a time sheet sweep every day. If this sounds over the top, the reality is that is not. It is quite a simple thing to automate, and it keeps your accounting section right on top of billings, giving you a daily view of potential cash flow and billing cycle trends. That ability to have that daily view, whether you use it every day or not, is an ability you will—at some point in your business growth—gratefully celebrate.

It is worth commenting here on an aspect of a growing consulting business that can compromise cash flow. Sometimes your client assignments can involve travel, which can be a significant expense. A typical mistake is for these expenses to be paid for on credit cards, and then not captured in the invoices to clients until after the credit card statements have arrived. Invariably, this results in your business having to pay the expenses before the client has time to reimburse the expenses, which means that your cash flow is funding project-related travel expenses. When you start your business, the expenses may be small and this issue may not be problematic. It is easy to overlook the need for early expense capture and invoicing.

However, as you grow and more of your staff travel on assignments, the lack of discipline in expense capture and invoicing can result in compromised cash flow. Consistent monitoring and recouping of project expenses require the same discipline as consistent monitoring and timely invoicing of time spent on projects.

The second way is to front end load your invoicing. Construction firms often charge a mobilization fee, which might be 10%, or 20%, or 25% of the estimated fee for the full job. This takes some edge of the cash flow risk. It is an urban myth that clients will not accept mobilization payments on projects from consultants. All you have to do is ask, and set out the terms clearly in your contract conditions. There is a little bit of quid pro quo in practice. Clients are likely to pay the last invoice only upon successful completion of the assignment, so the front-end loading does not mean that you get to invoice for the whole job before you actually finish it. But you can move a part of your cash flow earlier in your pipeline, keeping your cash-in-bank at healthier levels than they would be if you did nothing.

CREDITOR MANAGEMENT

Naturally, your business will owe money to others. In a consulting firm, these creditors fall into four categories. The first is your wages. Your responsibility as an employer will mean that you have no flexibility in how you manage the timing of your wages. Even if the statutory mandates requiring you to pay on time are weak, the moral mandates are very strong and the business reasons for paying wages on time are very compelling if you want an engaged workforce. Don't pay your people late, as you may never recover from that breach of faith. It sounds like an obvious rule, but it is a constant source of surprise to me how many employers feel they can bend this rule by a day or two.

Your second category of creditors comprises your subconsultants. These may be specialist services you bring in to enhance your services or to fill a gap in expertise. The most effective way of managing subconsultant invoices is to pay them only when you have been paid by the client. This is easier said than done, and poor discipline on your part—and on the part of your subconsultants—can lead to painful outcomes. Good discipline looks very simply like this: get your subconsultant to send their invoices to you just before you consolidate your invoices to the client, so that their invoices flow smoothly into your invoicing runs. Then shepherd the client payments through, as discussed in the previous section. And finally, when the client pays, pay your subconsultant promptly. If you maintain this discipline, you will find that you do not contribute to your subconsultants' cash flow stresses, and in turn they are more likely to be loyal and provide you with good service. Start paying them late and they are more likely to let you down.

Your third category of creditors are overheads such as information technology (IT) support, rent or lease expenses, and similar expenditures. A good rule of thumb is to schedule them to be paid when they are due, and not a moment earlier. And, because these overheads are either predictable or very trackable, it is smart practice to watch their accrual closely, to predict their trends and to ensure that you are setting aside funds for them each week.

The fourth category is taxes. You would be surprised at how many businesses fail to predict their tax bills or the timing of their tax payments. This is a painful mistake to make, and a simple one to avoid. Yet too many entrepreneurs, while correctly assuming that only a fraction of their income will be needed for tax purposes, neglect to manage their cash flow well enough to accrue the funds for their tax bills.

I used to work for a consultant—Bob—who, like me (but many years earlier) had started his own consulting firm and then sold it to a large multinational. Bob was a mentor, and was always generous with his advice. One of his recommendations, when I started my own firm, was to manage the finances closely. "Cash is king," he said. "Make sure you know where your cash is coming from and going to, every day. If you don't, then you're flirting with bankruptcy."

Personally, at the time, I thought that was one of the most boring, administrative pieces of advice I had ever heard. I was used to more visionary advice, and this just sounded like an accountant's Monday-morning monologue. It turned out to be the most important piece of business advice I have ever been given. Once you understand the cash flow at a weekly or even daily breakdown, the problem becomes smaller, the solutions more clear, and the sleepless nights fade away. Don't sniff with arrogance at the accountant's insight, as so many entrepreneurs are prone to do. Invest time in understanding the ebb and flow of cash. Develop a strong and frequent dialog with your accountant, and insist on frequent cashflow updates and projections. Look at those updates and projections carefully and cynically, seeking out the cashflow surprises that might be lurking there. There is simply no substitute in a growing business for good cashflow management.

As a director, you have a duty to ensure that your company can pay its debts as and when they fall due. Bob mused that most entrepreneurs forgot the last part of that duty—"as and when they fall due." "Timing," he said, "catches people out. You look at your invoicing and it adds up to a half-a-million dollars for the month. You look at your wages and it's only two hundred grand. Your expenses are less than fifty grand. You do the sums and you've got lots of float. And you do, if time wasn't a factor. But time is always a factor."

Before the global financial crisis, using lines of credit and bridging loans were common ways of navigating the timing factors inherent to cash flow management. In a way, relying on those mechanisms bred a relatively poor business discipline among entrepreneurs. Why watch cashflow like a hawk every week when a line of credit would bail you out for the short period of time you needed it to? It's lazy management and, while it may work sometimes, it gives you a false sense of control. You are not actively managing cash flow; you're merely using band-aid measures to navigate the dips and bumps. It's a dangerous way to manage your enterprise.

DEBT-FREE GROWTH IS NOT FOREVER

While the strategies outlined earlier, and some that you can probably envisage for yourself by now, take the sting out of cash flow management and support your efforts in debt-free growth, in my view they only delay the inevitable. At some point, you may need to either tone down your growth trajectory, because the pinch points are so dramatic, or seek other funding options to maintain your growth trajectory. If you project your business plan with a cash flow analysis and target your Exit Strategy, you will see exactly what I mean. Eventually, like death and taxes, the bank or some other source of funding becomes a reality if your Exit Strategy extends far enough out into an aggressive-growth future.

This book does not discuss debt-leveraged growth. Using debt is a perfectly viable strategy, and a very powerful one in its own right. It can extend the trajectory of your business growth much further than the horizon of debt-free growth and help to create an enterprise of even greater value than one without debt. It can unlock growth possibilities, including buying smaller firms to add to your existing enterprise. You can grow in jumps, mining the synergies between your core consulting firm and other practices to claim a larger market share or expand into new markets. The return on investment in debt-leveraged growth is more complex to predict and achieve than without debt, and it requires an investment mindset as well as a growth mindset.

As you near the horizon of debt-free growth, it is worth asking a question. The question is whether selling your company and reinvesting in something else is a better proposition than leveraging debt into your company and growing. The question is not just a financial one; it is also one that requires you to think about lifestyle and entrepreneurial independence. It is an important question to ponder and answer carefully.

THREE TIPS

Tip 1: Debt is a heavy burden for any company to bear, and—while it's not necessarily a grave mistake to go into debt—it is a good decision to avoid it where possible. And it *is* possible if you predict your cash flow carefully and watch it like a hawk.

Tip 2: Consolidate before you grow. Make sure you save the profits until you have more than you need for your growth steps. But remember, if you grow in cells, you have a greater chance of growing in small steps.

Tip 3: It is unlikely that you can keep growing indefinitely without going into debt, so understand that threshold well and, where possible, exit before you get there—or redefine your Exit Strategy and establish a new growth trajectory.

7

Partnering

Talent wins games, but teamwork and intelligence wins championships.

Michael Jordan

TO PARTNER OR NOT TO PARTNER

The question of whether or not to take on a partner, or partners, crosses most entrepreneurs' minds early in their musings about their consulting business. It is not a simple question to answer, as we will explore in this chapter. It is, however, worth remembering three statistics about start-up businesses that have two or more partners.

The first statistic is that the failure rates for businesses that have multiple partners at the helm, and businesses that have a single owner, are about the same. That probably implies, among other things, that if a business proposition is a poor one or its plan has a fatal flaw, it doesn't matter how many captains are piloting that ship. The second statistic is that, of companies that experience explosive and sustained growth, the vast majority are run by two or more partners. The ratio is between 4:1 and 10:1—depending on the type of industry studied. That is, four to ten times as many companies experiencing explosive and sustained growth are spearheaded by two or more partners, versus the number of explosive-growth companies with a single person at the helm.

The third statistic is that the arbitration, legal, and accounting industries in the United States and the United Kingdom are strong growth areas that witness annually increasing revenues from partnership breakdowns and the resulting activity required to reach settlement outcomes.

The threefold conclusion you might draw from this is that (1) start-up businesses will probably survive or fail on merit, not on diverse leadership, (2) partnering may harness some growth leverage that sole leadership is less likely to access, and (3) partnering introduces alignment risks that increasingly end in legal and financial rue.

So there may be both risk and reward in partnerships. Let's look at the pros and cons more carefully.

ADVANTAGES AND RISKS OF PARTNERING

Many partners I have talked to nominate the sharing of worry as their number one reason for partnering. This might initially be surprising, but when you look closer at the reason, it makes more and more sense. Starting a business is a stress-inducing activity. Quite apart from the financial stresses, the degree of personal and emotional ownership is very high. We—the human race—are a tribal people, finding a deep sense of comfort from shared endeavor. Should it surprise us then that business partnerships are quite often created from a shared vision and a commitment to a shared endeavor? This reason also gives us a vital clue about managing partnerships well, and this will be covered later in this chapter.

Closely following this reason, and perhaps even closely related to it, is the idea of synergy. Put simply, it is the acknowledgment that "you are good at that, and I am good at this, and we need both this and that to grow a strong business." This is an interesting and humble acknowledgment which, many arbitrators observe, often becomes lost as the business grows. In other words, the acknowledgment of strengths and weaknesses fades with time, especially as the business becomes more and more successful. A legal colleague referred to it dryly as the Pride of Kings—a phenomenon where partners' humility decreases with increasing business success, and the growth of ego crowds out the willingness or ability to recognize synergies. He offered no insight as to whether this loss of humility had any particular affinity with any particular gender, and whether or not there was an equally visible Pride of Queens in his experience. However, the identification of synergy—of a whole that is greater than the sum of the parts—is a very popular reason for creating partnerships, irrespective of whether the reason continues to be seen by all parties as the business grows.

Risk sharing is quoted by many partners, particularly in a financial context. If $200k is needed to start an enterprise, it may be better for you to find three others to share the capital input at $50k each, rather than finance it all yourself.

Closely related to risk sharing is redundancy, or backup. Starting and growing a consulting business can be a time-consuming venture. As a solo entrepreneur, especially in the first year or two, holidays are mere fables to tease your mind with, and you cannot afford to become ill. Lifestyle balances are hard to find, and regularly missing your children's events or your partner's important moments become a significant risk. Added to that, upward fluctuations in workload can leave you swamped and the necessary administrative functions of your enterprise can suffer. So having a partner or two to tag-team with can rebalance your life and reduce the risks that you may miss your children growing up, estrange your partner, or neglect your business' cash flow.

Across the board, especially in successful and long-lived partnerships, the strategic advantage created by diversity of opinion at the chief executive officer level was identified as an enduring strength. One very successful consulting legal entrepreneur, Carol, summed it up well. "The consulting market is flooded with small operators who have five or ten staff. Many of them are very talented and many with a strong service mentality that appeals to clients. A partnership of two has a better chance of outfoxing those smaller consulting firms. Good ideas survive, bad ideas are killed off. That kind of filtering can make you more competitive and more creative in the market." The old adage that two heads are better than one applies in consulting firms as much as it does to any other situation.

As a consulting firm grows bigger, the reach it has into the market—to identify and connect with new clients—becomes a significant factor in its growth. For most growing consulting firms, there is no brand recognition in the market place. Their logo is largely unknown. Introductions to the firm's advantages are often made in person by company principals, or transmitted by word of mouth via satisfied clients. Networking is an important part of growing a client base. The math is easy here. Two partners can network twice as much as one, and four partners can double that reach again.

Finally—and many partners do list this one last, although almost all partners I have ever spoken to specifically identify this one—there can be a great sense of camaraderie and fun in having a partner. It helps if your business partner is your friend at the start, but even if your business partner is merely a long-standing professional acquaintance, a strong friendship and a sense of camaraderie often eventually develops. This is unsurprising, as a shared passion and some aligned thinking is often a good enough basis for a friendship. Shared long enough, the friendship develops and deepens. But the key here, as many partners have pointed out to me, is that it is easier for two or three people to make genuine fun out of a business venture than it is for one person. A sole operator often has a sense of isolation, whereas two partners in business rarely suffer that feeling.

So there are, by many and varied accounts, tremendous advantages to partnering. But what about the risks?

Interestingly, I find that consultants in working partnerships are relatively blind to most of the risks. In fact, talking to them yields a short and frankly obvious list. The two groups of people with the greatest insights are arbitrators and consultants whose partnerships have endured difficult times or broken down entirely. Clearly, these people have had real exposure to the risks and consequences of partnering. Let us look at their top risks.

Number one, by far, is that partners diverge on business views. Arbitrators stress that this always happens. It is, in their view, inevitable that partners disagree at some point in the evolution of the business. The disagreements mostly occur in three areas—when and how to grow, how to administer the business and its cash flow, and (particularly for consulting firms) personnel issues. Most failed partnerships exhibit one common trait. They accrue a myriad of unresolved but smaller disagreements before hitting a significant tipping point. Arbitrators get to see this characteristic from an objective and fulsome perspective. Joe, an arbitrator whose bread-and-butter work is to untangle partnership woes, remarked "As we get deeper into reconciling the differences between partners during an arbitration process, the partners often each bring out past disagreements and grievances. These probably, at the time, seemed minor but in the light of a breaking relationship they become a cumulative grievance, and they add up to a very big set of differences developed over a long period of time." The inevitability of disagreement appears to be both a fact and a risk.

The second most quoted risk is that the stakes are high and therefore the emotions are high. Arbitrators point to the many consulting partnerships that have significant personal investments—professional, personal and financial—because the industry is one of knowledge, skills, and relationships. "When people feel that they have invested themselves into a venture, the stakes seem higher and it is difficult to separate feelings from facts. Objectivity can be lost and subjectivity can creep in," notes Joe. He recalls that a survivor of a failed partnership remarked "Looking back, we could have solved every one of those differences. But in the heat of the moment—for almost two years—we defaulted to conflict."

Finally, the risk that was referred to third most frequently was divergence on life balance views. One partner may wish to slow down, and another may wish to increase effort. Interestingly, arbitrators like Joe saw this—in practical terms—as quite a simple one to manage. "When one partner wants to slow down and the others want to speed up, the option most commonly taken is that the partner wanting a better life balance sells down some equity. Rarely does this transaction result in a failed partnership, although it has been known to happen."

There is a list of consequences that are relevant to failed partnerships, and it is worth keeping them in mind.

The cost of a failed partnership is high. It can be financially high, as significant business and personal resources can be directed toward finding a resolution. The survivors of failed partnerships liken the process to a bitter divorce, with lawyers' fees and accountants' fees taking a seemingly disproportionately high toll on personal and business finances. And the profitability of any business almost inevitably slumps, claim most arbitrators. Even when a buyout agreement is reached, the direct and indirect financial costs in getting to this point are considerable. The emotional cost is also high, with professional ties and friendships often damaged and destroyed along the way.

The period during which partnerships fail is characterized by partner underperformance. The conflict is distracting and partners are likely to be focused on resolving the conflict, to the point where the business mandate is not to grow or increase profits, but to "just hang in there." That partner underperformance, which often manifests as a disengaged management style, creates a broader fallout syndrome in the business. The dynamics of this can be quite visible, with staff taking sides, deeper rifts forming in the organization, increased absenteeism, reduced collaboration between consultants and, ultimately, lowered business performance. Market share can be lost, and credibility can be undermined. This can have a long-term effect even after the conflict is resolved, and even after partners buy each other out.

External to the business, the ripple may continue. Clients, who may have initially been sold on the synergy of the managing partners, will have individual views on which partner brought what value to the organization. These individual and different views will result in changed perceptions of the organization by clients. If one partner is bought out, for example, some clients may feel that the value lost by the consulting firm is sufficient to neutralize the strategic advantage it once had. Other clients may feel that the firm has not lost anything, and may in fact have gained something in the transition. Whatever the individual views, the collective group of clients accrued over the period that managing partners formed a cohesive force is likely to undergo some division.

A common outcome of split partnerships includes noncompetition clauses to prevent the partner that was bought out from competing with the remaining partners. This has the desired effect of excluding the partner who has been bought out from market transactions, but its effect in protecting the remaining partners is largely overestimated. In reality, the client division discussed earlier may result in a group of clients seeking their services from another competitor simply because they perceive a loss of strategic advantage. As one arbitrator dryly put it, "The partners may have forgotten the value that their synergy brought, but the clients sometimes don't have the same memory failure."

But what if there is unresolved conflict and it does not result in a failed partnership? "While that is something to be thankful for, it may be a hollow victory," notes Vikram, the organizational psychologist we met in Chapter 3. "Some conflicts result in winners and losers, and eventually the dynamic of winning and losing erodes trust between partners. Eroded trust makes your partnership less effective than it could be. So your partnership may not implode, but it may also not be as potent as it could be." The observation here is that while conflict is inevitable, the lack of rules of engagement and resolution may result in behaviors between partners that cross a line, breaking trust. The trust broken is not necessarily related to a financial or fiduciary value—it is more about interpersonal conflict, and how one or more partners navigate that conflict.

So the benefits of partnering can be significant, and so can its risks. How can the benefits be accessed while managing as much of the risk as practical? Arbitrators are almost universally supportive of all partnerships engaging in a charter of some kind. The charter reinforces three things. First, conflict is inevitable. Second, some future conflicts can be imagined, and many of their resolutions can be agreed in the early stages (the next section will discuss some examples to illustrate this point). And third, some conflicts that cannot be resolved can at least have an agreed path to resolution.

PARTNERSHIP CHARTER

Partners who have worked through conflict will tell you it is never too late for a charter—except, of course, when it really *is* too late! Conversely, it is never too early.

Where does a charter start? You can begin with your company constitution, and the operations of your Board. The company constitution has legally recognized status, so there are some governance issues that can be reasonably covered there. It will not prevent disagreements, but it can stop the disagreements from disintegrating the company.

One of the simplest governance tools is breaking a deadlock. Most partnerships, particularly in the consulting world, are two-person partnerships. A two-person, equal partnership has one significant Achilles' heel. When there are two strong opinions, and they are at odds with each other, a stalemate is reached. Decisions are not made, because if a decision is made there is a clear winner, a clear loser, and a shift in actual and perceived power. When decisions are not made, the dynamic nature of an entrepreneurial business is stunted. In addition to the obvious disadvantages of losing nimbleness in a market, staff can get frustrated with inaction, and a loss of faith in leadership can result.

A constitutional way of breaking the deadlock might include formal Board processes, and nonexecutive Board members, including a nonexecutive Chairman. The same applies to three- or four-partner firms, or more. A Board can help take the battle out of the partners' hands.

Many consulting firms run by partners balk at this notion. A Board takes away some control from the partners, which can be difficult for entrepreneurs who are enamored by the freedom of complete autonomy. Some argue that a Board is just a substitute for arbitration, and is more politically charged than arbitration. In reality, a Board supported by a simple but clear constitution can significantly reduce the risk of interpersonal battles between partners.

But a partnership charter goes much deeper than a constitutional and governance process, deadlock-breaking mechanisms and higher accountability. A good partnership charter should derisk a partnership significantly, even without a Board or carefully developed constitution. However, it should be remembered that a partnership charter is merely an agreement and as such, it is subject to the goodwill of all partners. Unless it is converted into a binding agreement or contract between partners—a move that can be quite stifling to a partnership, it is based on the notion that partners will respect and honor the charter.

Even though this sounds naïve, arbitrators observe that the notion is quite robust. A partnership agreement put in place when the points of disagreement are in the future and appear somewhat abstract—and the partners are thinking with cool heads—is surprisingly well-honored even years later, when circumstances have changed and decisions are made in times of stress.

> Roberto and Paolo recognized in each other very different risk-taking behaviors when it came to finances. Paolo had a much higher tolerance to risk, whereas Roberto was extremely conservative. At the start of their enterprise, the partners were still working out each other's boundaries. As the enterprise grew, and it needed to deploy working capital in growth— at the expense of operating cash reserves, Roberto recognized that they were heading toward disagreements. He estimated that they would start to have different opinions on how much working capital could be deployed in growth within the next 6 months.
>
> "So I rang up Paolo and said, 'we need to work out a framework for working capital use'," he remembered. "Paolo thought it was a good idea, so we left the office early one Friday and sat down in a café to work out this framework. We thought the rest of the day would be more than enough to do the job, and we had actually booked in a game of racketball in the late afternoon. In the end it took us 3 weeks to write a partnership charter that solved that issue, plus some others!"
>
> Roberto and Paolo found that discussing the problem, before it was a problem, without the stress of having to make an immediate decision, was difficult enough. Roberto wondered how much harder it would have been to address the issue the week or two before making a decision, with pressure on timing.
>
> In the end, Roberto said, they decided that their cash reserves would not be allowed to fall below 3 months' office rent and salaries for all staff. So any capital deployed would need to leave this much buffer in their bank account at all times. The discussion also allowed them to put in some agreed decision-making rules for how capital would be deployed. This formed the nucleus of a partnership agreement that extended to strategy decisions and, importantly for their eventual exit, agreement on how they would implement succession planning.
>
> "It was the best use of 3 weeks of our time, in all of the 12 years we worked together before selling the company," Roberto observed.

What should a partnership charter cover? The simple answer is, anything the partners like. At a minimum, issues such as growth, cash in the business and succession planning (in the case of a clean Exit Strategy) should be covered. Growth can include things such as which markets to go into and to stay out of, processes to cover expansions, debt-financing decision points, and so on. One partnership charter for a midsized accounting firm with four partners included the requirement to set out a business plan covering a number of mandatory points, critical review by an independent consultant, a follow-up report and addressing review points, and finally endorsement by the board for all expansions requiring more than $200,000 in capital. All partners had agreed to go through these hoops before expanding, and each partner could put up a competing business plan if they did not agree with another partner's business plan. The charter allowed for competitive thinking, with governance rules, and set the scene for business growth in a way that would not result in brawls between partners.

Cash in the business is quite straightforward, and there is almost universal agreement that it is the easiest issue to set agreements in partnership charters. The charter question that is often asked is "how much should we leave in the bank at all times in case something goes drastically wrong?" The answer is, almost invariably, a certain number of months of operating expenditures. Once crystallized, say many consultants, it is rare that partners argue about it in later years.

> "The four partners in our legal firm agreed that we would not grow until we had 6 months of operating cash locked in the bank, and thereafter all of our growth would be conditional on having 6 months' operating cash in the bank, no matter how big we were," Peter, a partner in a midsized legal firm explained. "In later years, this sum grew to quite a big number and admittedly we had one or two slightly tense conversations about unused capital. But it felt like an inviolable law we had created for ourselves, so we simply put the cash into mid term fixed deposits to create some value and held our principle. Each year, we used the interest from that reserve for our end of year party!" Succession planning agreements were, similarly, reasonably easy to define before the issue became a reality. "If anything," Peter says, "we set selection criteria that we probably would not have met ourselves, and processes for selection that in hindsight seem a bit controlling. And I know that at least one other partner feels that way. But it works, it is what we agreed to, and it keeps all partners happy."

Where succession planning is concerned, arbitrators observe that without some structure, the partners get into horse-trading about the values and shortcomings of various candidates, potentially creating division in the ranks below and polarizing the company. "Succession planning is a very political area," Don, a senior arbitrator who works for institutions of engineers in settling professional disputes, warns. "If you don't have clear and agreed means of accession and succession, staff can amplify the competitive nature of the issue, play one partner off against another, and damage the company from within. It's important to make the process both objective and agreed, and hold firm on it."

In addition to the three "must-have" aspects of partnering that many consultants with experience in partnerships (and arbitrators) nominate for the partnership charter, the list that you and your partner(s) may develop is entirely up to you. It is limited by your imagination, and there is no deadline for getting it 100% right. Don stresses that "while brevity is always a good thing, my experience suggests that writing down everything you can think of is better than trying to filter out the smaller things. The smaller things add up to bigger problems, and it's quite surprising how discussing the smaller issues can open up insights to the partners that may avoid the bigger problems. Remember, the charter is a living document. Don't write it during the Honeymoon phase and lock it in the safe to be pulled out when there is a disagreement. Some of the good practices I've seen include the partners coming together after Thanksgiving or before Christmas and revising their charter. It keeps the charter fresh and relevant, and allows the partners to include issues that are slowly creeping up on them."

WHAT PARTNERS?

Before selecting a partner, it is a good idea to think introspectively. At the core of self-examination is the question: would you make a good partner? An often-ignored fact is that some people are simply not cut out for partnerships. This is not a bad thing, necessarily—it just *is*. Ask consultants who have built their own firms without partners why they don't have a partner and you will get three common and interesting answers. The most prevalent one seems to be that it is just too much of a hassle. Some used the word *messy* to describe potential partnerships. They were not talking about the consequences of failure; they were referring to the effort it takes to make a partnership work.

The second most common response was this: *I'm too set in my ways to have a partner.* This is a refreshingly honest response. Many consultants who are ready to start their own enterprise have had several years in the workforce. They have worked with others and decided, after examining their own workstyles, that they are simply not the best team players. In many cases, this is quoted as the underlying reason they left a larger firm in the first place.

If this is you, starting a partnership could be a disaster in the making. If you are not likely to be flexible, to compromise, and to adjust your leadership style for a collective good, you are possibly the partner that other partners fear and, eventually, find too difficult to work with.

The third response was "I did it before, it was a disaster, and I would never do it again." This is a solid endorsement of the notion that if you get partnerships wrong, it can be a painful experience.

So, what if you are flexible and able to compromise, and you are considering a partnership? What should you look out for? There are a number of attributes successful partnerships exhibit in their choice of partners.

You are looking for a team player or team players. One(s) who shows the same flexibility and ability to compromise that you do. Start with the premise that you will have disagreement with your partner(s). The ability to discuss the differences, reconcile them amicably, and realign yourselves is critical.

You are looking for an equal. Pecking orders in partnerships are not real partnerships. Many legal firms have junior partners and senior partners, and they are not equal. There is a clear senior-to-junior division of labor, and there are lines of accountability—both formal and informal—that leave strategy at the senior level and delegate tactics to the junior level. There is nothing wrong with this model, but it is incorrect to think of it as a partnership model. The term "partner" is honorific rather than authentic. By equal, you are not looking for a carbon copy of yourself. You are looking for an equivalent ability in leadership, strategic thinking, and execution of strategy.

Ideally, you are also looking for synergy in skills and approach. Partners with complementary skills have a clear advantage over partners who have the same skill sets. More practically, unless you are Superman or Superwoman, it is highly unlikely you will possess all of the skills required to start, build, consolidate, diversify and sell a consulting firm. It is unlikely that the same brain that envisions growth prospects is adept at watching your cash flow. It is unlikely the same personality that can sell new services to new clients is able to nurture and develop employees over a long period of time. And if—despite its low likelihood—you *did* have all of these diverse skills, well, good luck finding *another* Superman or Superwoman!

Melanie, an organizational psychologist, remarks that partnerships are varied, and there is no recipe for an ideal partner mix. She points to two-person partnerships as being more common than others, and illustrates that differences and synergy can result in potent partnerships. "There is a reason that the Odd Couple complex is so popular in society. The dynamic between opposites—or more practically, diversity—yields high energy processes and outcomes. At the movies, that high energy is entertaining. In business, that high energy is creative fuel. Think Good Cop/Bad Cop, Nerd/Jock, Ice Queen/Mother Theresa and Brain/Brawn. Diversity at the helm can be very powerful. It creates divergent thinking, a natural advantage in the market. When leveraged well, only the best decisions make it through. Good ideas, following principles of Darwinism, adapt to become better and better as they are bounced between different partners until their chance of survival are optimized. Bad ideas become extinct. Don't be afraid of differences in partnerships—celebrate them."

Talk to the members of any successful partnerships, and they will present a long list of other attributes. Many of them are personal preferences—some of them quite specific—and that is the nature of partnerships. You will have your own preferred attributes, and they will depend on your own worldview. They are equally important because the partnership has to suit you. But no matter how many of those preferred attributes your potential partner has, never lose sight of the three that appear to underpin all successful partnerships—(a) find a team player; (b) find an equal; and (c) find someone whose skills complement yours.

FRIENDS AS PARTNERS

It is a very human question, and one that this section would be incomplete without answering. Should friends become business partners? After all, it feels like the partnership has a head start when the potential partners already get along well. Should friends jump into professional partnerships?

From a professional and business perspective, you do not need to be friends to have a very successful partnership. A shared vision and a commitment to executing sound strategy with a team player as strong as you, and with complementary skills, is a good recipe for success.

But is it an advantage? Every partnership I have seen that is strengthened by a bond of friendship has seemed to have a natural advantage.

'That advantage does not overcome an inherently weak partnership that might be uncompromising and unequal. If anything, the friendships are at risk of disintegrating along with the inherently weak partnership. But when a partnership is founded on solid business principles and enhanced by friendship, it can exceed expectations.

Why does it do this? Liam, a business coach who works with professional services firms and works with many consulting partnerships sees it this way. "If the business context, strategy and the partnership model is right, friendships add two things: depth and resilience. Depth, because friends are naturally inclined to communicate, and communication is the lifeblood of partnerships. Work out that communication muscle and you have strong, aligned leadership that explores issues in fine detail, resolves them soundly, and does this with the *enthusiasm* of working together; not the *reluctance* of working together that we often find in the workplace. Resilience, because friendship breeds loyalty, and vice versa. It is very hard for external or internal factors to divide loyal work colleagues because they stick together. All for one and one for all, like the Three Musketeers!"

Joseph, an engineer and tennis enthusiast who runs a large two-person partnership consulting enterprise with a close friend talks about trust. "I often think that a good two-person partnership is like good doubles tennis. There is intuitive two-way communication. Sometimes I call the play, sometimes Phil does. Where we are on the business court, our positions, how we adapt to each other's 'zones' is important. If Phil calls 'go right' I don't ask 'why'? I just go right instinctively. If I have a question, I reserve it for afterwards, and Phil does the same when the situation is reversed. It's fully reciprocated trust while we're in action, running our business, sometimes on different continents and in different time zones."

At a practical level, business partners who are friends spend more time together than business partners who are not friends. That extra time allows business partners to focus on the smaller details of their enterprise. Like the time that is required for craftsmanship, the investment can result in deep and subtle value injected into the organization. Some entrepreneurs point to attributes such as company culture, crediting the friendship between partners with creating unique and enjoyable working cultures that, in turn, attracted and retained excellent staff. Others point to client confidence, which appears to increase with the cohesion of the company's partners.

Uniformly across business partnerships, there is no evidence to suggest that partners who are friends is a bad thing, and plenty of evidence to suggest that there are strong and subtle advantages to friendships at the helm.

THREE TIPS

Tip 1: Spend a great deal of time in contemplation about your partner(s) before you choose him or her or them. A common vision is essential. Seek complementary skills so that the whole is greater than the sum of the leadership parts.

Tip 2: Disagreements will happen. Invest in a partnership charter that allows you to follow agreed ways of navigating them, and honor that charter.

Tip 3: Make sure you get along with your partner as a person. If you are at ease with each other, it multiplies your chances that your journey will be fun. If you are friends, you may create even greater value than your business plan suggests.

8

Stumbling

I like to make my own mistakes.

Mikhail Baryshnikov

Start a business and you will make mistakes. Run a business and you will make mistakes. Don't be one of the 90% of people who think that they will avoid mistakes. About 100% of them will be wrong. The business world is packed with factors that you and I have no control of. In fact, the business world is so saturated with these factors that you and I cannot hope to envisage all of them and plan adequately for all of them.

If any entrepreneur tells you that they strategized and executed strategy flawlessly, be cynical. Don't assume you can emulate this improbable achievement. You are going to make mistakes. You will learn from them, and become a better consulting entrepreneur. The trick is to make sure that the mistakes you make are not the ones that halt your enterprise or strip it of significant value. Like a ship's captain, you need to know where the reefs are, and avoid them. This knowledge will not save you from navigating into a squall or running into pirates, but it will save you from having your hull torn open on some sharp rocks.

In this chapter, we will discuss eight mistakes that have cost consulting firms their futures. To highlight the materiality of these mistakes—and often their innate foolishness!—this chapter will, for each of these mistakes, first discuss how you can increase your risks of making them. Hopefully, you will see some potential behaviors that you may be prone to, and you will become sensitive to them.

MISTAKE 1: IT'S ALL ABOUT THE BIG PICTURE

An excellent way to ensure your business fails is to be vague. Be vague about the value proposition you create. Be vague about the market, the clients, and the client sectors. Be vague about the types of consulting you will take to the market, and which cells you might develop. Being vague includes keeping your consulting model in your head so that it can wax and wane as it pleases. And for heaven's sake, don't write it down.

Why be vague? There are many good reasons. For one, vagueness is comforting. If we are undisciplined entrepreneurs, we might have a nagging suspicion that if we write down the details, some of the gaps will become evident. *This idea sounds better although it is slightly vague.* When we write it down, or become specific, the little bumps and wrinkles become evident. These little blemishes can be slightly demoralizing. The blemishes are also little, which means that they can be handled at a later time without too much fuss, *so why write them down?*

Another good reason is that "getting into the detail" seems less important than focusing on the strategy. This rationale is also quite true, which makes it a dangerous trap. If your strategy is wrong, no amount of specificity and clarity will improve it. But it is also true that many of the best strategies fail because they are not practical when they need to navigate the harsh reality of the detail. And that harsh reality remains blurry until we become more specific. Many entrepreneurs get caught up in the Big Picture. The Big Picture is, of course, vitally important. But it is made up of the little brush strokes that we need to peer at myopically if we want the Big Picture to be a work of art.

Today's commercial world of glib messaging has further downplayed the importance in business of specificity. Too often, we get caught up in the power of the Elevator Speech. We are taught that if we cannot encapsulate the business proposition in an Elevator Speech, there is a problem. In reality, if there is a problem with the absence of a great Elevator Speech, it may merely lie in the communication skills. If you cannot distil your consulting proposition into an Elevator Speech, do not sweat it. Conversely, if you have a great Elevator Speech, do not assume for a second that you have a good consulting business proposition. Whether it takes you a short elevator ride or a long train ride across Siberia to describe your consulting proposition, the most important thing is that it is clear and specific. It should be as clear and specific as your Exit Strategy, and you should be able to visualize it in excruciating detail. Saying it quickly and concisely in an elevator is a sales pitch, not a gauge of clarity.

To avoid the Curse of the Fuzziness, embrace clarity and specificity no matter how mundane it feels. Do not assume that, as the head of your enterprise, such detail and clarity is beneath you. If it is not clear in your mind, it is unlikely that it will be clear in anyone else's mind. And then both your direction and your destination are vague, and your consulting business is adrift. It may not flounder, but neither may it grow purposefully toward your Exit Strategy.

MISTAKE 2: PLANNING IS FOR GUMBIES

If you have managed people before, you may have requested a strategic plan or a business plan from them so that you could gain visibility and confidence in the direction your employees were planning to take. If you reported to someone, that person may have asked you for a strategic plan or a business plan, ostensibly for the same reason. In both cases, the strategic plan or business plan was used to evaluate performance in some way. Did you meet your plan? Did you exceed it? Did you fall short?

When seeking capital, the strategic plan or business plan lays out the reasons why the lender might want to (or at least be comfortable with the prospect that he or she could) throw some money your way. With the appropriate interest rate, payment plans, and collateral against the lending, of course.

In the business world, the planning document has become a communication tool, and a binding artifact to accountability. Often, the planning document is either intended to sell your pitch, or to leverage your remuneration, or to underpromise with the intention to overdeliver and get more of that bonus pool.

The business plan has become a piece of the game.

Your ego may tell you that if you are accountable to no one, then a business plan is pointless. A bit of a sketch of where you are going, neatly handwritten in a notebook is fine. After all, you know what you are doing. The business plan is for gumbies who are accountable to others, or who need some funding.

In a partnership, there is some accountability between the partners, so the requirement for a business plan might actually exist. Again, it may largely work as a communication tool. We just want to make sure we are all on the same page, right? Then we can put it on the shelf and go run our business in the real world.

So the business plan is just an administrative hassle. Why bother with any more investment in that process and document than the absolute minimum required to keep your stakeholders happy?

Abraham Lincoln once commented that if he had six hours to cut down a tree, he would spend the first four hours sharpening the axe. Your business planning benefits you the most if you first think of its role in that light. Like a commercial pilot who spends countless hours in a flight simulator before being granted a license, the business plan is your virtual training ground. It allows you to simulate the smooth running of your business, as well as your adaptability to turbulence in the business world and events out of your control. It allows you to simulate cash flow under a range of conditions to test your business resilience, and to ask what-if questions, then answer them. Yes, it is true that plans rarely remain intact after you begin the business in earnest. But while there is no substitute for operating your business in the real world, the business planning simulation exercises are the next best thing.

In-depth business planning, although introspective, bequeaths you perspectives that you would not have had before, without the pain of having to live through actual events in the business world. It gives you perspectives on what might happen if your client assumptions are wrong, or if your sales figures are 10%, 20%, and 30% less than your smooth-sailing business assumptions. It allows you to test your cell-investment strategies and to determine how prepared your business is to grow. It grants you insights into underlying cash-flow assumptions and resilience, painstakingly giving you implicit knowledge of where your limits of endurance are.

Done well, your business planning process is underpinned by scenario development and planning that charts your world in deep, if theoretical, data. It results in a likely or median path, plus and minus some elasticity, and some definition of your limits—how and when your business may exhibit signs of struggle, how and when it will struggle, and how and when it might fail.

Scott, an environmental consultant with a midsized national firm, described his planning this way. "I had never been a fan of planning but my wife, who is a banker, insisted I invest time and effort in deep planning. I found it frustrating at first, as I simply wanted to get on with the business, but I persevered. I must have generated dozens—maybe hundreds—of spreadsheets covering all kinds of scenarios—clients won, client retention, repeat work, the cost of hiring, salary costs, charge-out rates, fee discount models, bonus schemes, sector downturns, competitor success at lower-, middle-, and upper-end contract sizes and even the lengths and frequencies of my vacations! I spent time understanding the effect of each variable in isolation, then in combination with other variables. Then I wrote down the insights, one section for each element like the cost of hiring, in my business plan, and charted my target for the year. I would look at it each month, sometimes in earnest, sometimes just to re-familiarize myself with the insights. No one else except my wife (once!) ever looked at it. It was my compass. In the first year of my business, it felt like I had thought through just about everything that could happen, and I was very confident with my decisions. I liked the feeling so much that I now repeat it every year. I take a week out and re-run scenarios, update the plan, add new sections. Of course there are things that happen during the year that I hadn't foreseen—like a merger offer with a rival firm—but for the most part I was mentally 'in tune' with my business prospects each and every year, and I met or exceeded my growth and profit expectations every year."

Most successful consultants do their planning carefully, if nothing else to anchor themselves to a successful trajectory. Some consultants, like Scott, above, attempt to extract as much value from the planning exercise as possible. The choice of how much value to create and extract from a business plan is up to you.

MISTAKE 3: LEAVE MANAGING THE CASH TO THE ACCOUNTANTS

You are a professional, right? Your job is to consult, to lead your consulting troops, to develop business, and to control the quality of your company's outputs. Unless you are running an accounting consultancy, the bean-counting should be left to the bean-counters. Your job there should be to check the accounts monthly, survey the profits and the large expenses, familiarize yourself with where the money is coming from and nurture those pathways—and of course keep an eye on the liquidity of your company. Is that correct? The accountants should do the heavy lifting with the finances, ensuring that your books are kept up-to-date and your tax returns are filed according to the regulations.

That is, in fact, absolutely correct. And to borrow a phrase that scientists love to use, it is necessary but not sufficient.

The majority of businesses fail or become impaired not because their strategy is flawed, but because their cash flow is insufficient. Start-up and growth businesses are more at risk of cash-flow shortages because they are in a dynamic state. Cash-flow crises are in-the-moment crises, not strategic crises. Your billings may look admirable over a 1-year period looking forward, but it is the 1 or 2 months of poor cash flow that will undermine your business.

Assume, correctly, that cash flow in your business is as important as the blood flow in your body. Checking the accounts monthly (or quarterly, as some entrepreneurs do once their business is up and operating) is like pausing to check your pulse when you are running. You put two fingers to your wrist or neck and count out your heartbeats for 10 seconds. Everything feels right and you've done your due diligence.

But your role as the head of this enterprise, that is derived from your vision and fueled by your drive, is not to undertake due diligence in the perfunctory way that you might do for shareholders. It is not to merely *demonstrate to others* a duty of care. Onward!

Your role is to have a continuously running commentary on your heartbeat as you run. It is to have a heart-rate monitor to beep at you when your pulse rate exceeds or falls below some warning level, so that you immediately slow down or speed up as necessary to manage your cardiovascular effort adaptively. Your role is to monitor blood pressure in your body to ensure that you are staying in the safe zone, and within this the optimal zone.

Perhaps it is clichéd, but the term *cash is king* is, if anything, understated. Cash management—or liquidity management—is the single most important operational activity you can undertake. Take a cue from big businesses. Increasingly, company directors are being made directly and personally accountable for the liquidity of the companies they direct. One of their primary roles is to ensure that the company can pay its bills as and when they fall due. Analysts spend more and more time looking at the liquidity of a company, because they know that businesses with insufficient cash flow suffer a rapid but agonizing asphyxiation. And, as directors of more mature businesses observe, it is not all about creditors. It is also about having the necessary cash reserves to take opportunities in the market to maintain and increase the competitive edge that is so necessary to survival.

There are three tactics to keeping your cash flow strong.

The first is monitoring. Know your cash flow. Every day if necessary. Every week is good. Every month, if your cash reserves are strong—for example, if you have 6 months or so of operating funds. Any less frequent monitoring is dangerous. There are often collective groans when entrepreneurs are told this. There are dozens of reasons offered for not doing this—*administrative, time consuming, low-value, boring, small-picture, bean-counting*, and so on—and sadly, many businesses fall into the trap of being blindsided by a cash-flow crisis. Michael, an accounting consultant and owner of a midsized national firm that specializes in financial management for service companies comments that "your cash-flow monitoring should give you today's picture clearly, and it should inform you in detail of the picture over the next 3–6 months. It should tell you, to the nearest week, when your lowest cash-flow position will be. If you don't have this knowledge in your head, it is like driving with your eyes partly closed."

In practical terms, it is not hard to do. Consistent bookkeeping (once or twice weekly) is sufficient to deliver to you all the data you need to monitor cash flow. Specify the dashboards or reports to want your book-keeper or accountant to give you, and then spend time with them, regularly, looking for signs of strength and weakness, timing signals, improvement, or deterioration. It is an introspective task, but—like the insight you might get from watching your child play for an hour or two—it is exceedingly informative, and the knowledge makes you a strong entrepreneur.

But what if you monitor your forward cash flow, and it tells you that you may be heading for problems? That is where the second and third tactics come in.

The second tactic is controlling the timing of income and expenses. Although it sounds simple and intuitive, in our culture of credit many businesses incur expenses before they receive income. Timing is a simple and effective means of avoiding a problematic cash-flow dip. Your overall income and expenditures may not change, but the simple discipline of banking your income before incurring expenses can smooth away many cash-flow crises.

The third tactic—and one that entrepreneurs often hate hearing—is learning how to say "no" until your cash-flow position is demonstrably strong enough to say "yes." Say "no" to the office refurbishment. Say "no" to handing out corporate credit cards to your employees. Say "no" to business class flights for business development purposes. Do this with the understanding that these are temporary decisions pending the build-up of a strong, stable, and positive cash-flow business.

No successful business entrepreneur I have met has ever, in hindsight, rued watching and managing his or her cash flow carefully. None have confessed to me that the tiresome task of cash-flow management was a wasted effort. Almost all have agreed that it can feel boring and mundane. So if it feels like that to you, reflect that you are feeling just like many successful entrepreneurs before you.

MISTAKE 4: COMPROMISE YOUR QUALITY

It is normal, is it not, for your company to evolve from a low-volume, high-quality enterprise to a high-volume … how shall we put it … less quality-oriented organization. Provided you attract and retain clients, and you have a workforce that can deliver and maintain growth and profitability, does it matter if the standards that you first upheld become diluted?

This is a conundrum that consulting entrepreneurs deal with all the time—the gradual slippage of quality. A surprisingly large percentage of consulting entrepreneurs regard this as a simple fact of life, and appear resigned to some deterioration in quality. The conventional wisdom is that, provided the average quality does not slip below market expectations (in other words, our quality doesn't fall below everyone else's quality), it's OK.

I find it astonishing that consultants are willing to so easily trade off one of their crucial strategic advantages.

It helps to understand the forces that cause the slippage to occur. Typically, solo entrepreneur consultants are trading on their craft. Good craft creates a reputation, a brand that is associated with you. That brand is critical because, when you first enter the market, you need a differentiator. Unless your consulting credentials are already well differentiated in the market—in other words you are known as *the* best in the field—your market entry position might be "I can do that assignment as well as any, and for a slightly cheaper price (because I don't have the overheads of a big consulting firm)."

In time, with your quality credentials established, you might remove the price differentiator, because you are now selling (and have established, in the market) *value*.

When you grow your firm, and for some years during your journey, you may be the *sensei*, the head coach, the holder of the brand, of your firm. Yet, to grow, you must trust in the work ethic and quality of others, and you must delegate well. This process is gradual, as you wean clients off their reliance on your presence, and you build the capacity of your employees so that they emulate—and ideally surpass—the delivery that established your brand in the market.

The theory sounds good, but in practice the brand remains vested in you as the owner, and not your protégés. Your employees may not have the personal stake in the brand that you have, and therefore their diligence in maintaining or enhancing the quality of delivery may not be as high as yours. Under these conditions you might reasonably expect, as you grow, that others in your organization are responsible for more and more of the delivery, and that the average quality of delivery declines.

Colin, the consulting partner we met in Chapter 1 who gave up consulting noted that "after we had grown to a certain size, it was impossible to personally control quality. For example, I could not find the time to review every report that went out. I could not check the logic or the economic modeling of every assessment we undertook. Eventually, our work standards declined, the percentage of rework increased, and I became disillusioned."

Relying on principals and owners to maintain quality control only works to a certain point, because once the company is large enough, there is too much work being done and too much output being created for a sole owner or a couple of partners to be convinced of quality. So the next most senior people in the company become quality checkers. While this is better than nothing, unless that next level of senior people have a personal stake in the brand, there is some risk that quality will decline. Simple early signs of deteriorating quality include excessive use of cut-and-paste techniques (transposing solutions from another assignment onto the current one without structured and critical evaluation), insufficient evidence of project evaluation before commencement ("we've won the job, let's get stuck into it and finish it quickly") and informal peer signoff processes ("he/she agreed I was right, so I must be right").

Some consulting entrepreneurs use a filtering system to ensure that the quality of output sent to certain key clients remains high, by personally checking the output to those clients. So, "important" clients are serviced with informal but effective quality monitoring, and "less important" clients are not. It is a practical compromise, but still flawed. Brand attributes, and their deterioration, have a viral nature. If a "less important" client perceives a lack of quality, that perception will spread through the market, limiting your growth prospects.

To avoid this slow descent, it is important to plan the architecture of your growing company early and to allow for progressive implementation of quality management before you desperately need it. Your quality management must be simple and effective, and avoid overengineering or administrative overload. Every quality management system will be different, but there are three principles to bear in mind. First, make your quality management system risk-based. You do not need the same quality controls for simple or low-consequence assignments as you do for complex or high-consequence assignments. Second, carefully control and select the cohort of employees authorized to check and sign off—where possible incentivize those people to do their job well (or ensure there is a disincentive for them to gloss over their quality stewardship roles). And third, ensure that no output from your firm bypasses your quality management system. This last may seem so obvious as to not be worth mentioning, but most quality failures occur because quality processes were bypassed—not because the quality processes were inadequate.

Statistics tell us that most consulting firms will show observable quality declines over time, particularly in the first 5 years of growth. It is not that this trend is inevitable. It is simply that some optimistically believe that it won't happen to them, others are OK with it, and between them these two groups represent the majority of the market. You can be different.

MISTAKE 5: LET YOUR PRINCIPLES DILUTE WITH TIME

Most entrepreneurs start off with high ideals, but the practicalities of running a business force them to re-think those ideals. As they grow, and new staff come on board (with their own sets of ideals) it is natural for those first, idealistic principles to dilute. This is normal, and should be allowed for, correct? Failure to be flexible with principles will result in an autocratic organization that few will want to work for, right?

Although the argument has merit, it fails to recognize an important point. If your company successfully grows from, say, just yourself to, say, 20 people, it has done so because the principles at play have delivered successful outcomes. In a people-centric service organization like consulting, those principles are reasonably easy to identify. Typically, they are excellent client service, the delivery of promised quality on time and to budget, fair and ethical treatment of employees, and clear expectations and rewards.

At the start of the consulting journey, every client is precious to you. Consequently, service levels are high. Clients may see you frequently, they may feel continually informed and your discussions might be honest and guileless. At the start, when you only have five clients, each one is a significant part of your business. As you grow, and the number of clients grows, this individual recognition blurs. You may recognize the five or ten key clients who contribute 40% or 50% of your revenue, but the others are just that—*others*. Your client service might begin to display a kind of economic class system, reserving more time and care for the more valuable clients.

While this is a pragmatic and appropriate way to divide scarce client stewardship time, it is only productive if the *others* do not suffer from *inadequate* client service. Often that line is crossed silently and without recognition. Many consulting firms lose valuable repeat work from so-called second-tier clients, because they miss the point at which the line is crossed.

Guarding against this is not easy. Many consulting firms believe that if they repeat the mantra "the client comes first" often enough, it will become true. This is not so at all. In reality, client stewardship is part mindset and part discipline, quite possibly in equal parts. Checking in on a client regularly is a diary management discipline that is often lost in consulting firms. Some clients need their regularity to be more frequent, and others are satisfied with less frequent client stewardship. Capturing this information and translating it to regular client meetings, regular reviews of work in progress, and sufficient front-end thinking to create value are repeatable processes requiring personal and organizational discipline. And let's face it, not all clients are that pleasant to spend time with! So our very human response is to spend less time with clients we don't really get along with, and more time with clients whose company we enjoy. Recognizing and overcoming this natural instinct takes cold-blooded diary management and the discipline to carry it out.

Similarly, keeping promises—delivering to agreed time and quality—is one of the greatly undervalued characteristics of consulting firms. As an entrepreneur starting your journey, quality and timeliness are points of pride. As the company grows, tradeoffs start to occur. Quality and efficiency become exchangeable, rather than additive, commodities. Profitability is maximized if the quality is defensible rather than as promised, and the efficiency is the best it can be. This typically manifests itself in one of the biggest banes of a client's life—the consultant who sells the job on the basis of knowledge and expertise, then delegates to younger and cheaper consultants, ultimately delivering an inferior outcome than the sales pitch might have painted. And because younger, inexperienced consultants are overused in the project, it sometimes takes longer to deliver outcomes than the timeframe that was initially promised.

Speak to clients, and they will have many stories to tell about this somewhat seedy characteristic of consulting. It is the most prolific reason that clients change consultants. This very simple problem, which is intuitively known by all consultants, is hardly ever discussed in polite conversation, and it may be one of the reasons the practice continues to thrive. But it need not work that way in your organization. There is nothing wrong with seeking efficiency, provided it does not dilute the value proposition—the delivery and timing—that might have got you the contract in the first place. Keep your promises, and clients will come back. And, as we all know, repeat clients work like compounding interest in the background, growing your firm quietly but relentlessly.

The treatment of employees in consulting is no different to the treatment of employees anywhere else. If you want to attract and retain the best people, you need to treat them well. Small consulting firms sometimes start with a "small family" feel, in which norms are created around what is fair and ethical treatment. The norms vary widely. However, if you take your Exit Strategy view seriously and you understand basic human resource productivity, you may find that your norm naturally drifts toward the fairer, more ethical end of the spectrum. After all, you want to be able to relinquish control to a band of managers who will, through their own actions, attract and retain talent in such a way that your enterprise value is maximized. It may be a commendable end of the spectrum from an outsider's point of view, but you know that it also makes very good business sense.

How do you ensure that this clear-sighted business sense does not become unintentionally myopic as you grow? David, a Human Resource specialist, points out that there is more literature to read on this than could be assimilated in a lifetime, but puts it simply. "Consulting firms of fifty or more people have statistically one of the worst employee engagement scores across sectors. And yet, again statistically, if you interview the employees of much smaller successful consulting firms, employee engagement is often enviably high. So something is lost along the way. I ask consulting leaders to write down what they do when they start with their very first employees. And then, if what they are doing is successful and it feels right, to make sure they keep doing those things as they grow.

Often, these leaders simply forget what made their company great to work in when they only had modest offices and bad coffee. It's not that they changed or became less caring people. It isn't that complicated to remember what worked."

His reflection rings true. When building a consulting practice from zero, where every employee is a valuable source of client relationship-building and revenue, and every new employee is a substantial increase to operating costs, you put your best foot forward. You are leader and mentor, guide and protector, and your inner ethical compass is worn on your sleeve. You treat others as you would have them treat you, and you form a small nuclear family. Those family-oriented principles are important. It is very easy to replace them with organizational distance, systems, and processes that may retain legal fairness and gain clarity around expectations and rewards, but lose clarity around the principles you initially breathed life into. Those first principles can be your greatest ally as you grow, and your only—relatively simple—challenge is not to forget them.

MISTAKE 6: HIRE QUICKLY

Growth is exciting. Work floods in. Clients expect service delivery. If your resourcing is low, there is only one solution—hire. And hire fast. At face value, this is a good problem to have. The need to hire is, while stressful, also quite exhilarating.

The problem and solution are both familiar and seemingly inescapable. If you win work and you cannot deliver, you lose credibility in the market. A client does not want to hear that you were inadequately resourced for their project. So you have to hire, and you may not have the time to be selective.

The downside risk is that while you might solve a short-term problem, you may simultaneously create a long-term one. Your quick selection process might be flawed, and the person you hire may not be a good strategic fit for your future. Or your selection process might be good, but you had to recruit against your better judgment because the client service imperative overrode your misgivings. Either way, you may have inherited a short-term asset and a long-term liability.

There are two issues here, one about your personal level of comfort with hiring against your instinct, and one about your legal obligations. On a personal level, hiring with misgivings can be a nonauthentic transaction, and a disservice to both the employee and to your organization. If your misgivings are well founded, it is better to exit those employees and preserve the talent that you want to nurture toward your Exit Strategy. But if you fall into this cycle, hiring and firing reactively can create a sense of insecurity within your company, and your employees can, quite understandably, ask themselves whether they, too, were hired reactively, to fill a gap. That kind of insecurity leads to higher turnover as employees seek a "safer" environment in which to work. On a legal level, depending on the jurisdiction that you work in, the process of exiting employees can be long, drawn out, and sometimes contentious. Exits can be costly—in terms of settlement costs, management time, and the morale of remaining staff.

Recognizing that the growth you seek has this two-edged sword effect is the first step to managing it well in your company. If you are successful, you will face this problem. Therefore, knowing that you are going to be successful, how do you proactively put in place its solution?

Think of resourcing as drawn from three buckets, each deeper than the last. The first bucket is short-term contracting. Your margins on short-term contractors may be relatively small, but you can dip into this bucket quickly and easily, and you can withdraw from this bucket even quicker and easier. The second bucket is fixed-term employment. Your margins are somewhat higher here, especially if you can offer 6-month or 1-year fixed term employment. Breaking this contract may incur a payout of the remaining period of contract, but you know your liability at all times, and you can hedge your fixed-term agreements so that your liability is minimized. This presents the option of offering fixed-term employees more permanent, career-oriented prospects when you are comfortable—both personally and economically—with making such an offer. The third and deepest bucket comprises permanent roles. When you dip into this bucket, you should envisage that the person you choose is one that you would want in your company as you implement the final stages of your Exit Strategy. Consequently, your search and recruitment processes are likely to be much more considered, and to take more time.

With this model, do two things. First, build each bucket from the time you start your firm. And second, work through your resourcing triage in the order: bucket one, bucket two, and bucket three. Only move from bucket one to bucket two, and from bucket two to bucket three, when the pros outweigh the cons sufficiently to do so. This way your build—while admittedly slower than hiring quickly—is likely to be a more robust build and less likely to incur liabilities as you grow.

MISTAKE 7: WHEN THE GOING IS GOOD, YOU DON'T NEED BUSINESS DEVELOPMENT

Things are going well. So well, in fact, that it seems like a waste of time and effort to be doing too much business development; finding new clients and cross-selling within existing client structures. Why bother? And even if it didn't feel like it would be a waste of time, it's so busy right now that no one has the time and energy to develop extra business. And even if someone did, we would have far too little capacity to deliver any extra assignments, so that would actually create more of a problem. Ergo, it's better we don't do any business development. It would simply be a waste of time and effort.

So let's just get on with it and make hay while the sun shines, because it feels like the sunshine is going to last for a long time.

Which consultant, on a boom cycle of work, has not meandered through the will-I/won't-I circular argument about business development?

Despite being an obvious mistake to make, it is quite common among smaller consulting firms. Business development begins in earnest either when there is a downturn, or when there is a new cell to be developed. A downturn is actually the most competitive time, and therefore least efficient time to launch business development activities for two reasons. First, there is a downturn because work is drying up. Perhaps oil prices have dropped, or commodity prices have dropped, or consumer confidence is down and there is a recession in progress. Second, every other consultant is ramping up their business development activity. So, during a downturn, a great many contestants are fighting over a much smaller pie. Surely you should position yourself better during the more productive times to create a strategic advantage during the leaner periods?

The larger consulting firms avoid the mistake of overly cyclic business development by assigning business development personnel to hunting for work all year round, every year. Their task is to find new clients and new assignments, and feed them into the work pipeline. It is someone else's problem to deal with resourcing. The business development managers are incentivized by sales volume, and they generate very little revenue from their own advisory activity. They are, to a large extent, salespeople.

They are also an overhead cost, paid for by high volume consulting activity as a result of their sales. To carry such an overhead cost, your consulting business would need to be reasonably large and the sales generated by each business development salesperson for other people to undertake billable work would also have to be reasonably large. So how important or worthwhile is a business development specialist, and when is that specialty important for you?

A clue lies in the reason for business development. When asked why business development is carried out, almost 10 out of 10 consultants say "to make sales." And indeed, that is the practical outcome. But what creates the sales? Familiarity with brand and capability, confidence in management and trust. You can build these any time, without needing to translate it into a fee-earning outcome. You can build it to a level where a client opportunity (when there is one available) is more likely to translate into a fee-earning outcome for you than for your competitor.

So there is a good reason to maintain business development activity all the time. As an owner of your consulting firm, this should be on your agenda continually. It should be on the agenda of your senior personnel. And how do you do it? The same way you do client stewardship—with discipline in your diary. Set yourself goals of meeting a number of new clients and existing clients per month to keep developing your business, its reach, and its profile.

Many people ask if the tactic backfires. What if a new client offers you an assignment when you are too busy? You have three options. The first is to be honest and tell the client that the workload in your firm is very high and you could not do the assignment justice. In addition to being true, it wins you trust. A second tactic is to break the assignment up into phases, and only do an initial phase. This allows you to give the client a taste of the quality and delivery that can be expected, create a pathway to other (deferred) phases, and not overload your practice. And the third tactic is to take the project, send it down the line to more junior staff or someone who has a little bit of spare time (but perhaps inappropriate skills) and deliver uninspiring work. Don't let that "third-tactic person" be you, as this is a sign that you have forgotten what business development is about, at its strategic core—to build familiarity with brand, and to foster confidence and trust in management.

Think of business development as investing in your future, not investing in sales, and you will be more inclined to keep business development going continually whether you are in boom times or not.

MISTAKE 8: BUILD UP YOUR OVERHEAD

This is one of those mistakes that seems so obvious that it feels trite to even write it down. But it also feels negligent not to mention it! Everyone is in violent agreement that large overheads are a bad idea. Why then do overheads get away from us? There are subtle counterpoints to the notion that the only good overhead is a low overhead. What if you have dingy, badly-lit offices? Won't that deter clients, not to mention employees? Shouldn't office equipment be of a good standard? Shouldn't business development activity be strong and consistent, as opposed to being run on a shoestring budget?

These are fair points. A reasonable person would answer "yes" to all of the aforementioned. However, they introduce subjectivity and ambiguity. How much less dinginess and more light are we talking about? What is a "good" standard of office equipment? What do we mean by "strong and consistent"?

In the subjectivity and ambiguity, and in the search for the "right" answer, many overshoot the mark and overheads become a dangerous drain.

What, then, is the "right" level of overhead? In Chapter 5, we discussed the fees-to-salary ratio and the salary-to-total-cost ratio, which illustrate that sustainable overhead costs should be linked to sustainable fees-to-salary ratios. So there is no single right answer, but there is a sensible range that is dictated by your business mechanics. It is simple to identify from your accounts what this range is, for the past, the present, and the foreseeable future, and to institute controls so that you stay in that range. Following that, your only decisions are based on priorities. While staying within your overhead cost envelope, which overhead costs are more critical than others? This question is much easier to answer than the more ambiguous others.

THREE TIPS

Tip 1: Accept that you will make mistakes. Make every effort to avoid them, of course, but do not be so naïve that you think your strategy is bulletproof. Accepting the inevitability of mistakes improves your chances of adapting well to them.

Tip 2: Do not make the same mistake twice. Learn from it. Even better, do not make the same almost-mistake twice.

Tip 3: Learn from the mistakes of others. Watch consulting firms around you, and analyze their strategies. Others' mistakes are the cheapest education you will get.

9

Exit

I been a long time leaving but I'm going to be a long time gone.

Willie Nelson

INITIATING THE EXIT

If we were being philosophical, we would say that you had initiated your exit back at the point when you had conceived of your plan to create a consulting organization. However, the practical kick-off point of initiating an exit is when you begin signaling your intentions externally. I like to think of it as preparing to leave the party. You don't skulk away or make a beeline for the exit. That's just rude, and people notice you're gone anyway. You circulate, purposefully, in a general locus toward your hat and coat, but letting your friends and hosts know that you are thinking of going home. Hopefully they all say, "Oh no, but it's still early! Stick around, have some more shiraz!" But you continue, politely and relentlessly, toward the door.

It is important that your exit is not sprung as some last-minute surprise on your staff. You risk abandonment issues, loss of trust, general consternation, and a deep organizational worry that you are leaving a scuttled ship. From a practical perspective, you risk a greater staff turnover and loss of productivity, both of which stick out like a sore thumb to a prospective buyer.

Karyn, a broker who specializes in managing the acquisitions of service companies reveals that unless employees have been conditioned over months or years that an orderly sale will happen, the sale of a company can be a surprising and distressing transaction for them.

"Employees often come to know about a sale 2 or 3 months before a deal is struck. Sometimes it may only be as little 2 weeks. In many cases the preparation is secret and the announcement tends to be sudden. In those circumstances, productivity is lost and staff spend most of their time online looking for new jobs rather than being client-focused. In the worst cases, because of lowered productivity, the buyer revises the offer down and the seller is stuck in a no-win zone. The likelihood of the seller lifting productivity is low, and the buyer has the ability to push the price down further as the company looks more and more like a distressed asset. It can be quite a disaster, and the seller loses whether the sale goes through or not."

It is a sobering thought. You could spend years building a capital asset, and a lot of its value can be washed away in weeks or months. Yet it makes perfect sense. When your assets are almost entirely people, and when your customer proposition is based entirely on intellectual property, you are dealing with a potentially delicate sale process.

So there is no more important time for finesse than when you initiate the exit. There are three stakeholder groups that are critical to manage well at this stage. These are your staff, your clients, and your potential buyers.

Orderly, progressive communication with your staff is imperative. The most elegant exits are made when a potential sale has been common knowledge for a long time, and it is seen as a positive evolution rather than an ending. In smaller firms, this communication can be personal and inclusive, open, and even lighthearted. The essence of communication is this: you are not running away. *This is the plan, and it has always been the plan.* We have all known about the plan for quite some time now. These are the reasons. This is a good time to execute the plan. And the exit will happen for the right offer, with the right post-sale conditions, and acceptable impacts on employees.

There are three questions all staff will have: why, what, and how. If the "why" is understood and accepted over a period of time, the "what" and the "how" are much more easily dealt with. Conversely, if the "why" is missing or not understood, or if the "what" and the "how" are perceived to be unfair or inequitable, morale can break down quickly.

Your clients should know that you are considering a long overdue break from being captain of the ship, and again that it will be a process that is dependent on the right offer and the right conditions. In the meantime, it will be business as usual. It is only possible for you to make the latter claim if you are satisfied that your employees are responding well to the intent to sell. Client contact should ideally be in person, particularly with clients who have existing engagements with your firm. It can be unsettling for a client to receive an email about an impending sale while he or she is sweating on the delivery of an important assignment. If the sale process occurs over weeks or months, regular contact and updates are helpful. These will convey to your clients and your buyers that client commitments are important to you, and that client stewardship isn't declining in inverse proportionality to your personal wealth! Maintaining goodwill with clients and buyers is important during the sale process.

Prospective buyers should know that you have an intention, but not an imperative, to sell. In other words, you are not desperate. The market should know that you are on a steady growth path. You have a stable workforce, and your management, in particular, is strong and effective. Your firm is profitable and diversified. In this regard, timing is everything if you want to command a good sale price. If you cannot authentically project these characteristics into the market, lower your expectations about your sale price, or wait and keep working on your business until you can demonstrate them.

Of course, it's not always possible to program your exit this way. Other factors outside of your business control, such as ill health, can lead to a rushed exit. You could have a recession in multiple sectors that causes your clients, and therefore you, to feel the economic pinch. But if you have grown your business systematically toward this outcome, you can initiate the exit strongly, with plenty of cues, direct signals, and indirect signals into the market, to underpin a smooth transition.

PREPARATION

In chess, a game of strategy, good players devote 90% of their moves toward subtle positioning and preparation before the final execution sequence that leads to checkmate. Selling your company is no less strategic. David, a specialist in mergers and acquisitions, reflects that "Most acquisitions happen with a sense of urgency. Naturally, all parties want to reach a conclusion as soon as possible. Once a counterparty is engaged, you want a short window to either make a deal or re-open the deal to other parties. That's appropriate. But acquisitions don't have to be initiated urgently unless there are factors forcing the acquisition. Many sellers seem to miss that point, and jump in with a sense of 'hurry up and sell.' Often this is just a personal imperative, driven by impatience. I start by asking 'do you really have to sell?' in order to figure out whether we can go slow and strategically, or whether we are really working against a clock."

Capture your strategy in a report. Write it in simple language for a broad audience. Pretend that you are explaining your business value to a group of shareholders, not to a seasoned consultant. Imagine you are writing a prospectus. Your buyer may operate a consulting firm similar to yours, and he or she may be very familiar with the types of activities your firm undertakes. But your buyer may also be represented by a broker, or may be looking to vertically integrate their existing business with yours, or merely seeking a productive asset. In other words, their inherent understanding of *your* strategy may not be deep or sophisticated. Your preparation should include a clear articulation of why your type of business is needed in the marketplace, why your particular business stands out in the market place, what your strategy is, how we know you are being successful with the execution of that strategy, and why the current status of the company offers growth potential on one or more trajectories. This document should transfer the exciting vision in your head to your buyer's head. It should create a sense of excitement about the prospect of looking at your business. Don't try to sell what you don't have, because any effective due diligence will expose this quickly, and your negotiating credibility will be undermined.

While setting out your strategy is your opportunity to differentiate yourself and excite, your accounts should be set up to soothe and calm the buyer. Set up your accounts, especially your profit and loss account, balance sheet, debtor history, and cash flow analyses, to be clear and transparent, and compile them for at least the past 3 years; 5 years, if you can manage it. Put yourself in a buyer's shoes and ask yourself if your books show the trends in the bulleted list below. (It is often useful to have a commentary on each year's accounts addressing these questions, because it will save potential buyers from forming a negative or ambiguous first impression of the strength of your business.)

- Is there a strong underlying growth in earnings or revenue?
- Does the underlying growth in earnings show smoothness, or are there anomalies such as large one-off contracts that you need to explain in the books? If you remove anomalies, is there still evidence of underlying growth in earnings?
- Are your earnings spread across a large number of clients? If they are, are those clients spread across a number of sectors? If they are, are

those sectors largely independent of each other? How much repeat work, over how many years, are attributed to the various clients? Can you demonstrate client loyalty?

- What is your profit, in absolute terms and as a percentage of revenue? Do both show growth, and at the very least does your absolute profit grow while your profitability (profit as a percentage of revenue) remains steady or grows?
- What is your cash flow position over time, and at the moment? Does it show continually increasing strength and resilience over the previous 3–5 years?
- What are your total salary costs, partitioned by base salary and bonus incentives? Are they at market? Does the distribution of bonuses confirm that your revenue and profit successes were planned, rather than being some fortuitous accident?
- What is your work-in-progress (the amount of billable activity in the forward pipeline) and does it show a growing pipeline each year? Is the pipeline growth at least equivalent to or stronger than your total salary cost growth?
- What is your debt level? Are future debts and liabilities laid out clearly? Have you been scrupulous with these, including rather than excluding doubtful items? Have you avoided any sense that you are hiding something?
- If you have multiple offices, reflect as much of the above as practical in your office-by-office financial breakdown. Can you show a pattern of geographic revenue and profit growth? Which offices are stronger and weaker performers? Can you show a pattern of strengthening previously weaker performers, highlighting that your strategy works for the parts as well as the whole?
- What is your management structure? Is the development of this structure evident from looking at the previous 3–5 years? Does the structure resonate with your vision and strategy? What is the tenure of each member of your management team? Why are they a good team for the present and the future? What are their salaries, bonus incentives, and shareholdings (both current shares and share options)?
- Where is your talent in the organization? Who are the star performers below your management group? Do you have talent depth for succession planning?
- Reflect on whether you have spoken enough with your staff. How will they feel as you initiate the sale process? Have you invested as

much time as necessary in keeping your staff safe and comfortable? What's in it for them? Have you got them anticipating the change with excitement?

- Take a look at yourself. Are you mentally and physically in shape for what might be an intensive time in your life? Do you have the capacity to carry out two jobs simultaneously: one fulfilling the role you currently undertake in your firm, and the other negotiating a sale? Both will feel like full-time jobs if you want to do them well. Do you have the emotional support of friends and family to go through the sale process? Are you ready?

ACCESSING BUYERS

The first thing to remember about buyers is that the more there are, the better it is for you.

Having said that, let us pause for a moment on the alternative prospect of selling within the company. The simplest, and quite common, sale proposition is when existing partners buy you out. Obviously this is only possible if you have partners (see Chapter 8). The sale process can be relatively simple, largely because all partners have a similar and detailed view of the value of the company. Negotiations occur just like any other sale process, but the negotiations are usually quite pointed and pragmatic. After all, there is no courtship process, and there is very little point in trying to "dress up" the company for sale.

Another internal sale proposition is the management buyout, in which your subordinates or management team buy you out. This is always a possibility, but not always practical or the most profitable way to exit. A number of factors hamper its sale value. First, and most obviously, as discussed in Chapter 1, your staff may not have access to capital. They may have their own families and mortgages to support, and personal capital may be a limiting factor. It presents challenges for you, the seller, when negotiating. Many of the staff members on the other side of the negotiating table may be valued employees of yours, and it takes a certain ability to dissociate yourself from the personal and professional relationships you may have had. Put simply, it's very hard to hardball people you are familiar with. It is not impossible, but neither is it everyone's preferred negotiating environment. Second, and less obviously, greater prices are commanded if there is a way to grow the company after purchase. However, growing a company rapidly usually requires capital, and your staff would need to access two pools of capital to justify a higher price—capital to buy you out, and capital to grow. The probability of success in securing a high price is consequently slimmer. Still, many consulting Exit Strategies do proceed by way of management buyouts, and it may be a viable option for you. It does have the advantage of not having to search too far for a buyer.

If you are seeking an independent buyer, there are two broad options. One is to hire a broker, and the other is to go direct to the market. The two are not mutually exclusive or independent, and both can occur concurrently (although some brokers balk if they know you are doing both). In either case, it is beneficial if you, the seller, know who your potential buyers are. This kind of intelligence should not be left to a broker if you want to guide the destiny of the sale process to some extent.

Mapping potential buyers allows you to gauge the size of the market and, more importantly, segment your buyers by value proposition. Buyers have a range of motivators, and these motivators have a bearing on an individual buyer's value proposition. Some buyers, for example, may want to buy you out primarily because you are a competitor. They may have strategic ideas about the market, and you happen to be a thorn in their side. Buying you out gives them your market share, which is all well and good, but perhaps more importantly it allows them a clearer sweep of the market.

Other buyers may want to vertically integrate their value propositions in the market. Your niche might fit into their value chain, allowing them to consolidate market offerings to clients and take a more commanding position in the market. And others may want to simply diversify to give themselves more market spread, greater access to various sectors and increase the resilience of their own business. Others may envy your cash flow and profitability, seeing a "cash cow" proposition in the making. Some buyers might be in it for personal reasons. Some buyers may be looking to break up your company and sell some parts to buyers that they might know; others may want to grow rapidly and "flip" your asset in 5 years for a lot more money. Overseas companies may see the acquisition of your company as a quick and effective market entry ploy into the country or countries in which you have offices. Your negotiating and selling strategy can be usefully informed by such insights.

Because you know your market well (or you would not be in the position you are in!), you can segment your potential buyers and ask, putting yourself in each buyer's position, "What would I do with this company if I bought it?"

How is segmenting done? Not dissimilar to a stakeholder analysis, map out who might be interested. A spreadsheet is useful. Think of concentric circles to define your geography in widening arcs, for example, This City, This Country, This Region, and The World. These may be the columns in your spreadsheet. Now think of the primary reasons for buying your company—Remove Competition, Vertically Integrate, Diversify, and so on. List them in the rows of your spreadsheet. In each box, list the likely companies who might be interested in your firm. You may be pleasantly surprised at how rich this "long list" of potential suitors is.

Next, research in a little bit more depth the companies that have recently been active in the mergers or acquisition market. Consolidation happens continually, although there may be waves of consolidation that are quite obvious. Note the companies that have acquired smaller firms recently, and note the types of firms that have been purchased. Look at their competitors. Have they done the same? Are they likely to do the same? Look at client lists of all the companies that you are honing in on. Are they similar to yours? Are they complementary, between sectors, within sectors and geographically? In other words, do some of them list Coca Cola as their client, and you have Pepsi? Do some have a strong mining contingent, and you have a strong oil/gas contingent? Do some cover Nestlé in Africa, while you cover a subsidiary of Nestlé in South America? Do they fit in a vertically integrated value chain?

Finally, look at the money. Which companies have good cash reserves and/or low debt leveraging? Listed companies have this information publicly available to meet shareholder disclosure regulations, whereas unlisted companies are much less likely to show their hand.

This kind of research takes months, and if your Exit Strategy has been front-of-mind for years, you will have done some of this thinking for a while now. But this is the time to distill all that thinking into a picture of the market as it is today.

At the end of this process, you will have a shortlist that comprises companies you should definitely approach as well as companies that you probably should approach. You might rank them if you have the insights to do so. If you are just starting out, you may feel that you do not have those insights, but in my experience, most leaders of consulting firms develop these insights over time. Trust that you will, too. If the list is long, consider a broker. If the list is short, consider a broker anyway—they often add value. However, depending on how much time you have and how confident you are in your own brokering abilities, you might decide to proceed on your own.

If you decide to approach a broker, walk in with your list and the research that supports it, organized into a target pack covering the *who* and the *why*. Don't be embarrassed if you think your research might be lightweight at this stage. It will almost certainly be better than any insight the broker might be starting off with, because you have compiled that list with careful consideration of the specific value your firm might offer those companies on the list.

And while it might be tempting to excitedly jump on the first offer you get, fight that temptation. If a broker tells you that they have someone who might be interested, this may well be true. But you will be doing yourself a favor if you suggest to the brokers that they contact you when they have three or more potentially interested parties. Or five, if you are patient enough and your circumstances allow it. Remember, while the first offer has every possibility of being the best offer, that is not what statistics tell us. As David, the mergers and acquisition broker we met earlier in this chapter observes, "Supply and demand is a simple and generally bankable mechanism if you have the time to allow it to work for you. You are supplying one thing, and you would like as much demand for that one thing as possible to drive the price up. Competition from buyers is your friend. It can push prices up 20%, 40% or even 100%. It almost always results in a better outcome for the seller. When you sell, you should ask your broker quite seriously how you can start a bidding war."

If you choose a broker, make sure that the sale value and complexity of your business is roughly in the midrange of the types of sales they handle. If yours is in the bigger end of their business, they may be stretched to provide you with the best advice. If yours is in the smaller end, you may not get the service you hoped for. And while there are exceptions to this sweeping generalization, this is *your* endgame, so set the field how you would like it to be. Shop around for your brokers. If you have done your market homework, you are not paying for their market insights as much as you are paying for a front office to approach, attract, and process potential buyers. You are paying for external facilitation so that you can keep running the business and looking after your people.

Look at a broker's fee structure. This may be either a fixed fee, a percentage of the price or—in many cases—a hybrid of the two, much like a retainer and success fee model. If you are using a broker, be creative. You do not need to accept a boilerplate fee structure. Brokers are negotiators by trade, so negotiating with them is often perfectly acceptable. Suggest a win-win fee structure that incentivizes them to give you the best outcome.

If you are not using a broker, you have some decisions to make about your time management. Maximizing the number of viable buyers at the table takes time. There is some cold-calling involved because not every buyer quietly contemplating expansion has signaled a readiness to enter the market, and so they are invisible. In addition, negotiating is usually protracted and iterative. If you think it will take 3 months and occupy half your time, be prepared to double that estimate. It may take 3 months with all of your time, or 6 months with half of your time to work through negotiations, and not many buyers will have the patience for longer time frames.

Paolo, the owner (in partnership) of a consulting firm whom we met in Chapter 3 reflects on his sale process this way: "We went selling for 3 months without a broker, and realized that we would either have to put in a lot more of our own time and effort into the sale, or risk accepting a mediocre outcome, or get help. But we wanted the right kind of help, so we were very specific about exactly what we wanted a third party to do. In the end, the sale happened in 6 weeks without consuming our time as it had in the previous 3 months."

Nicolas, who sold a PR firm to a larger advertising agency, did not go to an open market. He said, "I knew who was interested in my company about 3 years before I sold it. The buyer initially approached me with an offer, which I declined. It was too early, and I had some growing to do. I kept the lines of communication open, worked on my business with them in mind and approached them nearly 3 years later when I was ready. We were quite familiar with each other so the discussions progressed quickly. The sale—between the first phone call I made and the settlement date—was concluded within 8 weeks."

―――――――――――

MANAGING YOUR PEOPLE DURING THE SALE

Most people fear change. It is a natural reaction. It is neither a sign of insecurity nor irrationality. Nor is it a blind fear of change. It is a dislike of vulnerability. If change is on the near horizon, we are programmed to move into a mode of high alertness. This alertness has us asking questions that we may not have asked before. The questions, if unanswered, create ambiguity in our lives. Ambiguity erodes our sense of security. When security is removed, we feel vulnerable. And nobody relishes feeling vulnerable.

If you have built your consulting firm, and if you have guided its development over some years, like it or not you are to some extent synonymous with your employees' feeling of security. Even if you have successfully devolved responsibility to your managers and you are a slightly expensive overhead, you have hardwired yourself into your company's DNA, and extracting yourself may be uncomfortable at a cellular level. Keep this in mind, if not for human reasons, then at least for economic reasons.

In Chapter 2, we identified the ideal timing of a sale as being a point at which the growth trajectory is still upward. Depending on how stable your market is, you might confidently forecast this based on a strong growth run. However, the productivity of your people can quite easily flatten out or reverse that trend in the time that it takes to complete a sale—typically a few months. When that happens, your firm can transition from being at the optimum point for sale, to a suboptimal point. Buyers are acutely tuned into this phenomenon. They are quite adept at recognizing its signs and revising their offer downward, when they see those signs.

Pete, a lawyer who specializes in mergers and acquisitions of service companies, puts it this way: "Even if the effects are not apparent in your accounts yet, if your business development outcomes falter, if the turnover of personnel increases or key people leave, if client references show that quality is on the decline—these typically trigger renegotiation. All of these indicate that the key assets of a service company—its people—are not operating where they should be."

Two things may happen next. The buyer's offer is reduced, or the golden handcuffs come out (or they get tighter, if you haven't achieved your Houdini-like maneuver of becoming mostly redundant). Often, both price reductions and constraints occur.

How do you avoid the reduction of your firm's value as a result of people risk? Throughout this book, we have been highlighting the value of your people. They are your greatest asset. Their creativity, ideas, effort, client stewardship, and the outcomes they generate are your source of revenue and your reputation. How do we optimize this in the lead up to the sale?

Ben, a former McKinsey partner, draws parallels to selling your car. "When you sell your car, what do you do to maximize its sale value? You replace older, worn tires. You fix the scratches and dents, maybe clean the interior and the engine. You service the engine and tune the suspension. You make adjustments, big and small, depending on what condition your car is in."

It is not a bad analogy, even if it is not very human! It makes two important points. First—and this is often a point of discomfort—you replace old, less efficient parts. For your firm, this may mean looking objectively at your people. Do you have too many people for the output your firm creates? Are there areas of consistently low effectiveness or efficiency? If there are, and if you have people who are reducing your firm's productivity, it is often better to remove them from your firm well before sale. This is for two reasons. One, a more efficient and productive firm will be more attractive and generate better offers from more confident buyers. Two, those adjustments to people will be made eventually—if not by you, then potentially by your buyer. Removing people from your firm will, in most circumstances, cause a ripple of uncertainty for your employees no matter when it is done, and no matter how well it is done. That ripple creates a sense of vulnerability for people. It is best to have that ripple out of the way well before you sell, and to present your organization with the strongest employee morale you can muster before sale.

The second important point is one that we have touched on throughout this book. Your people are prepared. Engineers and mechanics call it preventative maintenance. You have been anticipating the sale for a long time, and it comes as no surprise to your employees. Your communications have been growing more frequent and specific over the last few months, or even the last year or two. Your people feel less vulnerable because they have been thinking about a sale for some time, even if at a very low level. They have "rehearsed" it in their minds, and you have over time given them the script. Your objective is this: as you approach the point of sale, all of your current employees should be anticipating an improvement in their lives. They should feel that they are going from good to better. Minimize feelings of vulnerability.

If you think this is easier said than done then you are correct. Like most things, the theory is easier than the practice. But it is harder if you leave it too late, and easier if you do it in small, consistent steps. And that is your job as the leader. While the transformation from your early days to your point of sale might be large, you have always known where you are going. The journey might be long, but you have made small, almost leisurely steps, toward your destination and your people have felt safe.

If you have systematically eradicated inefficiency and your people are not feeling vulnerable, you have placed yourself in a good position. Your company is resilient. People are less likely to become spooked and leave. But what would make them stay, as opposed to simply not going? How do you create reasons for people to stay?

Without knowing who the buyer is, and what the post-sale opportunities are, it is very difficult to be specific about the upside of a sale. But because a buyer is likely to want to create a return on investment, there is a good chance that the sale of a robust asset results in a generally upward trajectory in growth, diversification, revenues, and profits. The same, of course, cannot be said for a distressed or suboptimized asset.

While this can create a sense of optimistic anticipation to counter the very human feelings of uncertainty, it may not be enough.

In Chapter 2, we discussed briefly the advantages of having your management team all-but-running the firm at the point of sale (with some potential equity stake to give them "skin in the game"). This is an effective strategy, and one that is welcomed by many buyers. It does not increase how much they have to pay for the company (although the non-financial value of the company might be increased, in their eyes, by the aspect of management shareholding). It may make your discussions internally more protracted, but this can be limited by two things. One is ensuring you (or you and your partners) have the majority or supermajority shareholding; and two is ensuring your company constitution and voting rights allow shareholders to hold value but not powers of veto that might hamper a sale.

In addition to shareholdings, you may set aside a completion bonus on sale for your key employees. The key employees might include senior management and certain pivotal individuals whom you do not want to leave. A completion bonus might be payable some weeks or even months after settlement, and this can further stabilize your firm's personnel mix during the sale process. Naturally, the completion bonus does impact your balance sheet, as it is an expense provision that will be taken into account during valuation, but it can easily pay for itself by minimizing the risk of personnel leaving during the sale process. Many sellers introduce a completion bonus in the year that the sale is anticipated to occur, and this often crystallizes in the minds of your employees your intention to sell. Done early enough, it is instructive to employees in a way that broad communications often cannot match, and sets a measured tone for entering into the sale process.

RESPONDING TO YOUR PEOPLE'S NEEDS

In the previous section, we discussed mechanisms of preserving value in the business during sale, recognizing that your employees are your biggest (and often only) asset. However, it is very difficult, at the start of your enterprise, to imagine what the exit might feel like to people some years later. While the aforementioned mechanisms and tactics are good business practices, it is worth dwelling on the human element of this period. Thinking about them deeply enough will help you institute the above advice well, and it will also help you anticipate and manage the less quantifiable issues of change.

It is very hard to project how you and your people will feel toward the end. Imagine a grandparent trying to explain to a teenager the responsibility and joy that raising a family brings. The grandparent might be quite impassioned about it, and might even explain it quite well. But, while the concepts of responsibility and joy may sound plausible to the teenager, he or she might not be able to appreciate the depth of personal and emotional connectivity this implies. So the explanation might sound believable, and the teenager might acknowledge that his or her grandparent actually means what is being said, but the teenager is unlikely to walk away from the conversation converted, and itching to start a family! The grandparent's point, while plausible, also seems slightly abstract.

You, like me, and like almost every successful consulting entrepreneur I have met, are quite likely to underestimate the impact that a sale will have on people in your firm. And you might even underestimate the impact it could have on you. There are exceptions to every generalization, of course, but it is prudent to assume that your case is unlikely to be exceptional in this regard.

In Chapter 3, we discussed the importance of picking your consultants well. We discussed the strategic benefit of grooming key people to, collectively, take over your mantle. Because consulting is a people-oriented industry, where your prime assets are intelligence and emotional quotients, your coinvestment in these two assets is considerable. Good consulting leaders are mentors. They teach you how to think insightfully, how to interact in the way great service organizations to, and how to combine both successfully. Good consultants are protégés. They learn from their mentors, adapt the learning and brand it with their own personal style. The coinvestment—leader to protégés and protégés to leaders—can be significant, if you are building a genuinely successful consulting firm.

Intellectual and emotional coinvestment binds people together. If you do your job well, you will retain many staff over long periods of time. Your first protégés may be there at the point of exit. Over this period of time, that coinvestment accrues. And, at the end, parting can be daunting.

Many consultants reflect, quite honestly, that the strength and purpose of an Exit Strategy makes the parting less daunting than it could have been. *"Yes, it was sad to sell, but that was always the plan so it wasn't like a shock or anything."* And that is quite correct. However, your coinvestors—your protégés and your staff—do not benefit from the strength and purpose of an Exit Strategy. Even those protégés that you may have groomed for the future have not had the length of time that you have had to internalize the Exit Strategy. So you have a natural emotional advantage at exit. If it feels slightly sad for you, assume that for those that do not have that advantage, it may feel deeper and more intense.

We have dealt with productivity issues above, and let us acknowledge that they are pragmatic business considerations. Many entrepreneurs point out that the purpose of a business is to create shareholder value. This is not incorrect. If your business has a number of external shareholders, like a listed company, then you have a prime fiduciary obligation to those shareholders to create that value, and productivity is a significant part of value creation. If you are the key shareholder, then you have a somewhat greater flexibility to determine what your primary obligations are. And one of those might be empathizing with and reducing the emotional impacts on your staff.

Helen, the successful consultant we met in Chapter 3, reflected that "it felt like a family. After about 3 years, we had a warm and personally invested culture. When I was planning the details of selling the business, I found that the hard-nosed business focus I had was mixed with an equal or even greater focus on the welfare of my staff. I mean, I was always caring, but as we started working toward a sale I slept less, I worried more about how people were feeling, and they worried about each other, and worried about me. We were heading to an exciting future, but we were a worried company! Even clients noticed. It was frankly quite surprising. I wasn't prepared for it."

This is the downside of a good corporate culture. When change comes—and it must, because change was the purpose of beginning your enterprise—people are affected. And while you can put in all the appropriate measures to preserve business value during the sale, what can you do to reduce the effects on people?

Unsurprisingly, many successful consultants and organizational psychologists agree on the solution—simply be present. Few successful consulting entrepreneurs recognize their own iconic status among their staff. That status is powerful, and its power is exercised simply by being visible. Brand consultants know this effect intimately. Recognizable icons simply need to be present in the right context. You, as the CEO seeking to depart, can be made more visible. Rarely has the phrase *management by walking around* been more appropriate.

"It takes an incredible amount of time," David the M&A advisor admits. "We find that the issue is not so much that the leader doesn't want to do it. It is just that the leader didn't realize it would be such an important thing, and did not factor it into the sale plans. And even if the time was factored in, the intensity of the sale process was underestimated, so the leader takes less time to sit down with the employees in formal, semiformal, and informal connections."

What then could be done to address this issue? Karl, the conflict resolution consultant we met in Chapter 3, says it is as simple as acknowledgment of the issue, a willingness to address it and the commitment to change in order to do so. "I realized that the legacy I left behind in the company was in large part about how people felt. And since I had never been through a sale process before while leading potentially anxious staff, I sought help. I used a business mentor. It was like having a personal trainer for the 6 months it took to sell the business. I changed my habits, waking up earlier to review sale documents and contract changes, I went to the gym every morning, ate differently, quit alcohol, set aside family time, slept early. It gave me the time and energy to travel to my offices and walk around for 2 hours each morning and 1 hour each afternoon, every day, and connect with staff. I think it had a positive impact on them. It certainly had one on me."

Karl's point, however he chose to act on it, was that he recognized that it was a unique and pivotal time, so his mindset was to have a unique— and quite holistic—approach to making time to connect with his people. The vast majority of employees who have been through a period of change agree. "You appreciate a leader who is there, who talks authentically, and who is there for you—not just for himself," Jane, a business consultant who was one of the midlevel staff in a consulting firm that was sold to a larger competitor, observes. "I reflect that the sale was well handled just because I felt OK about it, and I would work for our CEO again in an instant if he asked. To be honest I can't remember the hundreds of details from that time, even though they felt important at the time, but I remember him walking around, sitting down, making time for us, asking questions, answering ours."

Jim, an elder statesman who had made a wildly successful exit a decade or more before I had started thinking about an enterprise, recalled to me once how he'd initiated his exit from a successful firm whose consulting business was undertaking capital feasibility studies. The signals, he said, had been loud and clear for almost 2 years. He had been taking more skiing trips, and he had always come back remarking that he could do skiing trips all year. He had started taking Wednesday afternoons off for golf and turning up politely late on Monday mornings. His presence at Board meetings was benign, he said. "I vaguely disagreed with half the decisions made, but they were trivial disagreements, ones that did not materially affect company culture or value, and it was important that the leadership of the company made decisions that were not heavily influenced by me."

Nonetheless, he recalled, his conversations were universally met with anguish by his staff. "But you're too young to retire!" was the most common protest he received.

Despite all that he'd done to signal his intentions, his staff went into a phase that he called "pre-mourning." Jim's observation was this. In a happy culture, self-induced change can be menacing. Why change if all is good? Or, more pointedly, things are perfect now, any change can only be for the worse. Jim's experience was, I thought, the perfect manifestation of the two-edged sword of elegant exits. I asked him how he handled it. "I spent a lot of the next 8 or 9 months circulating and talking, checking in on projects, showing people that I was still interested, I still cared, even if it was time for a change for me," he said. "And I told them their future was in their hands, not mine."

DEALING WITH BUYERS

Connecting cold with buyers only works when the market conditions favor you. In other words, there is a demand for your kind of firm, and you can magically appear in the market and be welcomed. This rarely happens, particularly if you are seeking to sell on your own terms, in a planned manner, and not as an opportunistic transaction. You enter the market when your business is in a good position to be sold, and the market can be either hungry for your type of business, relatively ambivalent, or outright disinterested. From a practical perspective, expect the market to be relatively ambivalent but willing to become interested. In any free market, except in the most dire of economic circumstances, there are usually buyers for a real value proposition, which means you need to dial up your intentions at an appropriate pace.

When you are ready to sell, you should have already identified your potential suitors, and you should have already had many courtship meetings during which you have signaled that you will probably sell in the not-too-distant future. This is priming the market. You want as many buyers interested as possible, and your job is to gather that interest. If you prime the market well, the price goes up, and the deal gets done quicker. If you only have one buyer, be prepared for a more laborious deal and be prepared to settle for a lower price if you really want out.

It is hard to know what to expect when engaging with a buyer. At the heart of it all, it is a negotiation. You want the highest price, they want the lowest. There are other things you want—stability for your staff, a sense of continuity, the safe handover of a brand, and client stewardship. They want stability too, but they will want change. Systems might change to their systems. Roles in your company might change to roles that complement existing structures they have. Some buyers will approach the purchase with finesse, while others might be clumsier. None of these are things you can control, although your advice will be mostly welcomed by an astute buyer. No one wants to spook the horse they are about to ride, and you—the leader—knows the horse best.

Buyers can increase the speed of negotiations, and it is prudent to be prepared for it so that you, the seller, do not become flustered. A sense of urgency on the buyer's part can contribute to this. The timing of a large contract, for example, can influence how a buyer approaches you. If a buyer wants the sale complete before the profits from the large contract start to come in, things can get heated. In a negotiating sense, this can work to your advantage, but the temperature in the kitchen can be more intense than you'd planned for.

Whether amicable or hostile (and most deals are on the amicable side of average) you have an advantage. You are still the captain of your ship, and you should shield your charges from any turbulence that the sale process brings. If you have shared the equity around well, your sale team includes the key people in your organization. They are part of the negotiation, which can take the pressure off you, but also increase the complexity of the negotiation process. But unless you are a minority shareholder, the negotiation is largely about financing you to leave for a different life. So you are a key stakeholder.

Buyers balk when you display reluctance at their reasonable requests, or are sluggish in meeting their requests. Recalling the importance of good preparation, accounts should be produced promptly. Interviews with key personnel should be scheduled quickly and with minimum fuss. Treat the sale like an important project and prioritize it. Anticipate what will be asked for (they will be much the same as the things you would ask for if buying a firm like yours!), and have these things ready before you initiate the exit. The sale process can move very quickly if you're ready. No buyer wants to make an offer, then have another buyer make a better counter offer. A bidding war does not suit a buyer; it suits you, the seller. So buyers typically move quickly when the proposition is good, and get distracted if the pace becomes too sluggish.

Having an intermediary can be advantageous here. The sale process can make your life frenetic. A broker can filter and organize buyer requests so that you can settle the pace and allow time for your staff and your business. A broker can also manage some of the more unreasonable requests. Buyers come in all shapes and sizes, and some could be more personally invested than others in the transaction. The more personally involved they are, the more specific and pedantic some requests can become. There have been examples of requests to interview each and every person in an organization to gauge its culture and its willingness to adapt; of psychometric testing to be carried out on senior and middle management; of requests to prepare detailed manifestos of business development activities and opportunities per client and per sector; and so on. These are examples of requests that, unless underpinned by a very specific reason, can be much more than conventional due diligence and business-as-usual assessments. A broker can be very useful in moderating these requests, saving you the time and the frustration of either arguing about them or working late into the night to fulfill them.

Finally, your face-to-face interactions with buyers are important. Because it is your firm, your verbal and nonverbal cues are the subject of much interest. How confident are you? Are you calm or tense? Do some questions rattle you, and why? Are you on time? Are you prepared? Are you unavailable or over-available? Unlike the acquisitions of larger enterprises where there is no single senior manager of note and larger executive management teams come under broad scrutiny, there is quite an intense spotlight on you—the iconic leader/shareholder. This means that how you prepare yourself personally—the last section of this chapter—is important for the sale process as well as for you.

Many entrepreneurs who have sold willingly have remarked that the stress they endured during the sale process seemed to have been more than it should have been. Horst, a consummate entrepreneur who executed his sale process over a period of 6 months, then disappeared off the face of the earth to recuperate for nearly a year. He was surfing remote beaches around southeast Asia and the Pacific. When he returned, I asked him how the process went.

"It was actually very straightforward," he mused. "I think most of the stress was self-generated. I agonized about giving away 5% here or there. In fact, I took every negotiation point as a slight on the company value.... The company I valued, my baby."

"Isn't 5% worth fighting for?" I asked, already knowing the answer.

"Well, yes and no. Yes on principle. And yes in practice. In hindsight though, a 5% move in the valuation doesn't reduce my future options by 5%. It doesn't dent my plans at all. So yes, negotiate hard, but not to the point where you lose perspective and take things personally. You're about to become independently wealthy, plus or minus 5%, and if you can avoid the need to de-stress for a year as a result of that happy outcome, you probably should."

STEWARDSHIP OF YOUR CLIENTS

Of the three groups of people we consider in this chapter, clients seem to be the least flustered by a sale process. You do not want them to find out from someone else, of course, but nonetheless it can seem quite surreal to you when you gently spring your "big news" on them over lunch and they are more interested in telling you how much they like the great facelift the restaurant had since last year!

But of course, that makes sense. If you've done your job well, executed strategy well, you're the person they occasionally have lunch with, the person who asks for frank feedback and then (hopefully) does something subtle to achieve some kind of continuous improvement in service. At this stage, the only thing they may associate you with is lunches and philosophical chats, maybe some strategy, some less-is-more input that might be greatly appreciated but only digestible (and affordable) in small doses. You may be no good to talk detail with; you lost that ability with them a long time ago. So when you sell your company, the potential for any adverse impact on their projects may feel reasonably low.

Still, the reassurance from you that nothing changes, delivery of assignments is paramount, and service is second to nothing is essential. If you weren't doing the rounds and satisfying this simple hygiene protocol, there would be something wrong, something fishy. It is one of those things that no one may thank you for doing, but many might criticize you if you did not.

The exit conversations with clients are, in my experience, the most relaxing of all. They ask if you'll consult back to them. You say (regretfully) that this will not happen for a while because you will not compete with your old organization (and your buyer will probably insist on this in the sale contract anyway). Some of them will tell you of a role in their organization, or offer you a job. If you do it right, you should walk away warm and fuzzy, and with a deep sense of wellbeing, from the exit conversations with clients.

In the cynical world in which we live, buyers can be quite touchy about the prospect of you doing the rounds with clients during a sale process. They may worry that you are saying something inappropriate to clients that might, in the future, impact on client confidence in the new owners. They may also worry that you are squirreling away future prospects of work with these clients. It is prudent to discuss your intentions and provide the right assurances to your buyers that your client interactions during the sale process are being carried out to preserve value for them. It may also be professional courtesy, and a symbolic handing over of reins to the senior members of your firm that they may have been dealing with in the past. Some buyers may insist on sending along their representatives with you, and the appropriateness of this is quite dependent on individual circumstances. Where it is a contentious issue, a broker can help ease tensions.

YOU

Having done the rounds of the key stakeholders in your exit, let us focus now on you. If that sounds self-indulgent and a bit Millennial, take comfort from the fact that it *is* all about you. This phase is the realization of your vision, your Exit Strategy and your relentless efforts in getting here. It is your endgame.

The single most common observation from successful entrepreneurs who have sold their companies is this—*it was an intense period.*

So let us be Zen about this and work on your mind, your body, and your spirit.

Mentally, prepare to be resilient. Hostage negotiators are prepared for ebb and flow, for give and take, for agreement to be reneged upon, and for the unpredictability of the kidnappers. If they went in expecting everything to go smoothly, it is a very stressful job for them. Mentally, hope for the best but plan for a bumpy ride. If it is indeed bumpy, you can say to yourself, "Ah, I told you so. Lucky I came prepared, eh?" And if it is not bumpy, you can slap yourself on the back and have a leisurely mental cigar.

Your mindset should be that of a Formula One driver entering the last lap. Exhilaration at being out in front, watchful for unanticipated problems, avoiding mistakes caused by lapses in concentration, focusing on staying out in front, driving relentlessly toward the finish line.

Selling is latently frustrating because you expect you'll get a good price for your firm—your pride and joy at this point—and your buyer expects to get a bargain. It is unlikely that the number in your head matches the number in his or her head. If expectations are the roots of all unhappiness, then your expectations here risk causing you some annoyance. Think of the range you will be happy with—an acceptable lower bound and a pleasing upper bound—and you will relax a lot more on this ride. Have one single round number on your mind and—well, prepare for that number to change, and do not grind your teeth too much while it is changing.

Get rid of other worries while you are selling. Do not add stresses you do not need. Don't, for example, start negotiating the purchase of a house while working on your sale. Ensure that you are not working on complex projects in your firm; this is a time to have fully delegated consulting activities to others. Avoid other big events and decisions in your life if you can, and focus singularly on the sale. This is your Exit Strategy in action; you have prepared for this for some years now, so play it purposefully and with as much undivided concentration as you can muster.

No matter how mentally prepared you are, stress accumulates incrementally. Stress affects your health, and poor health exacerbates the effects of stress. Stay healthy. Start a healthy routine 2 months or more before you begin the sale process, and stick to it. Plan your meetings around your health regimen. There are three things to manage—sleep, nutrition, and exercise. You might be surprised at how quickly your sleep patterns can disintegrate during the sale process; how many times you wake up at 2 AM thinking, unable to go back to sleep. Look up those evening routines to improve your chances of undisturbed sleep and use them. Find a regular bedtime, even though it can be tempting to burn the midnight oil repeatedly poring over the fine print of an offer.

The stress of the sale process can have you defaulting to too much coffee, sugar-rich food and junk food, throwing your energy levels up and down like a yoyo—precisely what you don't need when you are trying to concentrate on offers, counteroffers, and legal advice. It's an easy loss of discipline though—there is so much going on during the day, and often so much to review during the nights, that irregular, poor meals become part of the intense landscape of the sale process. Karl, the conflict resolution consultant, anticipated the pressure the sale process would put on his body, and acted strategically. "I consulted a nutritionist because I wanted an elevated level of energy throughout the day, but I didn't want to be buzzing at night. I wasn't sure how long the sale would take, so the diet had to work for several months. I mostly followed the nutritionist advice, and I found I was sharper than I had ever been as a consultant! My clients had missed out on my best and most productive period because I was on my way out!"

The twofold demands of running the company (with whatever remaining management input you have) and navigating a sale process requires a healthy metabolism. The days are long and the workload feels about twice as much as you have ever had to cope with. Mentally, you are in high gear, and your body needs to keep up. Paul, a successful consulting entrepreneur who sold his business after an 18-month process, swears by exercise. "I kept fit by going to the gym or surfing, usually early so the activity didn't eat into my day. And, when I was too distracted for either, I would take long walks in the evenings to think through decisions I had to make. Over an extended period of time, my fitness gave me an edge that I would not have otherwise had. I was waking up earlier and sleeping better, despite the craziness of that period."

However you choose to do it, maintaining your health is an activity you probably won't regret. If the least it does is prevent you from having a heart attack, it's worth it.

To navigate a sale well, you want to be able to think objectively. This requires a certain amount of detachment; a mindfulness that allows you to weigh up options clearly, negotiate evenly, and avoid being frustrated. You need to be in a good place within yourself, or you will find the sale process excruciating. Think about it—you have spent several years building, from the ground up, a firm that you have envisioned. You have carefully crafted something, instilling in it a deep sense of *you*. You have brought in employees and guided them to take over the business; to be as good as or better than you ever were. And now you are selling it. It is a wrenching time, even though you have prepared for this from the very start. Opposite feelings collide—sadness at selling something you have invested so much of yourself in, and exhilaration at a plan well executed. This is a time to be centered, clear on your purpose, accepting of the conflict and mindful of keeping your tranquility as you go through the weeks and months of the sale. It is a time to keep other turbulences at bay; other life challenges that might distract you from executing this last part with precision and style. Pick the time to sell, if you can, when other parts of your life are in relative balance. And if you cannot, then keep the company of good friends and family to help you maintain your center.

I have seen many entrepreneurs finish the sale process looking like they have been through a wringer. I have known some who have become ill, and one who has had a heart attack. The intensity of this time and its toll on you—mind, body, and spirit—can be a recipe for burnout. Many people I have known, once the sale is over, take a long holiday—and it seems that it is less of a celebration and more of a recuperation for most of those people. Underestimating the sale process is a mistake that many people make; don't be one of them, and look after the center of this saga—you— as best as you can, and as best as your good friends and family can. And remember, you wrote this story from the start. You write the ending. How you exit is largely up to you. Make it a graceful one.

Index